The WordPress Troubleshooting Guide

Fixing Common Website Issues

Tasvir Mahmood

Tasvir Media Press

ISBN: 9798856889870

Cover design by: Art Painter
Library of Congress Control Number: 2018675309
Printed in the United States of America

Dedicated to all WordPress users

CONTENTS

CHAPTER 1: INTRODUCTION TO WORDPRESS TROUBLESHOOTING

Welcome to "The WordPress Troubleshooting Guide: Fixing Common Website Issues." In this introductory chapter, we embark on a journey into the world of WordPress troubleshooting, exploring the significance of this skill in maintaining a healthy and functional website. Whether you are a beginner or an experienced WordPress user, understanding troubleshooting techniques is essential to ensure a seamless user experience and the smooth functioning of your website.

A well-maintained website is crucial for attracting and retaining visitors, and this is where WordPress troubleshooting comes into play. Website issues can arise for various reasons, such as theme or plugin conflicts, coding errors, security vulnerabilities, or server-related problems. Troubleshooting involves the process of identifying and resolving these issues to restore your website to optimal performance.

The Importance of WordPress Troubleshooting
WordPress is a powerful and versatile content management system (CMS) that empowers millions of websites around the world. However, with the sheer number of themes, plugins, and customizations available, it's not uncommon to encounter challenges that may affect your website's functionality. This is where troubleshooting becomes a valuable skill to have in your arsenal. By mastering the art of troubleshooting, you gain

the ability to diagnose and address issues effectively, reducing website downtime and potential loss of visitors.

The Role of Troubleshooting in Website Maintenance

Website maintenance is an ongoing process that involves regular updates, backups, and security checks. In this context, troubleshooting serves as a fundamental component of website maintenance. Instead of being reactive to issues as they arise, troubleshooting allows you to take a proactive approach to spot potential problems before they escalate. By promptly resolving issues and understanding their root causes, you can keep your website running smoothly and provide an optimal user experience to your audience.

In "The WordPress Troubleshooting Guide," we will equip you with the knowledge and techniques needed to navigate through common website issues efficiently. From identifying error messages to analyzing logs, debugging code, and applying preventive measures, this guide will cover a wide range of troubleshooting scenarios to empower you with practical solutions.

Whether you're a website owner, developer, or someone responsible for managing WordPress sites, this guide is designed to be accessible and informative for users of all skill levels. With each chapter, you will gain valuable insights and actionable steps to tackle specific website issues confidently.

As we proceed through the chapters, you'll develop a troubleshooting mindset and adopt a systematic approach to problem-solving. Remember, troubleshooting is not just about fixing errors; it's about gaining a deeper understanding of your website's intricacies and ensuring its stability and functionality.

Now, let's dive into the world of WordPress troubleshooting and embark on a journey to become adept at resolving common website issues. With the knowledge you'll gain from this guide, you'll be well-prepared to overcome any challenges that come your way and maintain a thriving WordPress-powered website.

CHAPTER 2: UNDERSTANDING COMMON WEBSITE ISSUES

In this chapter, we delve into the realm of common website issues that WordPress users often encounter. Understanding these issues is vital as it lays the foundation for effective troubleshooting and resolution. By familiarizing yourself with the challenges that website owners frequently face, you'll be better equipped to diagnose and address them efficiently, ensuring a seamless user experience for your website visitors.

Website Performance Problems
Website performance is a critical aspect of user satisfaction. Slow website loading times, lagging interactions, and unresponsive pages are some common performance-related issues. We explore the factors that can contribute to poor website performance, such as hosting limitations, large image sizes, excessive plugins, and poorly optimized code. By understanding these factors, you'll be better positioned to implement the necessary optimizations and enhancements to improve your website's speed and responsiveness.

Compatibility Challenges with Themes and Plugins
Themes and plugins are the backbone of WordPress customization, but they can sometimes clash and cause compatibility issues. In this section, we explore how conflicts between themes and plugins can lead to broken layouts, dysfunctional features, or even website crashes. By identifying and resolving compatibility challenges, you can harness the full potential of your chosen themes and plugins while maintaining

a stable and harmonious website environment.

Error Messages and Troublesome Alerts

WordPress often communicates errors and issues through various error messages and alerts. These messages can be cryptic to the untrained eye, making it essential to understand their meanings and implications. We examine common error messages, such as "404 Not Found," "500 Internal Server Error," and "Connection Timed Out." By deciphering these messages, you can gain valuable insights into potential problems and undertake the necessary steps to resolve them effectively.

Security Vulnerabilities and Hacking Attempts

Website security is a paramount concern for every WordPress user. Understanding common security vulnerabilities, such as weak passwords, outdated software, and insecure plugins, is crucial to safeguarding your website from potential threats. We delve into the types of hacking attempts WordPress websites may encounter and explore best practices for enhancing your website's security, protecting sensitive data, and maintaining user trust.

Content and Media-related Problems

Content is the backbone of any website, and issues related to its display and integration can hinder user engagement. Problems such as broken links, missing images, or improper formatting can affect the overall user experience. In this section, we discuss techniques for addressing these content-related challenges and ensuring that your website content is delivered accurately and compellingly to your audience.

SEO and Search Ranking Issues

Search Engine Optimization (SEO) plays a pivotal role in driving organic traffic to your website. However, common SEO issues, such as duplicate content, broken redirects, or improperly configured sitemaps, can negatively impact your search engine rankings. We explore ways to diagnose and rectify these SEO-related challenges, helping you optimize your website to achieve higher visibility and attract more visitors.

Mobile Responsiveness Challenges

In an increasingly mobile-oriented world, ensuring that your website displays correctly on various devices is crucial. Mobile responsiveness issues can arise due to coding errors, incompatible plugins, or unoptimized media. We delve into the intricacies of mobile responsiveness troubleshooting, guiding you to create a seamless and engaging user experience across different screen sizes and devices.

In conclusion, this chapter equips you with an in-depth understanding of the common website issues encountered in WordPress. By comprehending these challenges, you'll be better prepared to address them systematically in the subsequent chapters. Troubleshooting website issues requires a keen eye for detail and a thorough understanding of WordPress functionalities, both of which we will develop throughout this guide. With this knowledge, you'll be well on your way to becoming a proficient troubleshooter and maintaining a healthy, functional, and user-friendly WordPress website.

CHAPTER 3: DIAGNOSING WORDPRESS ERRORS

In this pivotal chapter, we embark on a journey into the art of diagnosing WordPress errors—a critical skill that forms the backbone of effective troubleshooting. Diagnosing errors involves identifying the root causes behind common website issues, allowing you to implement targeted solutions and restore your website to peak performance. Through a systematic approach to error diagnosis, you will gain the confidence and expertise needed to tackle a wide range of challenges encountered in the WordPress ecosystem.

Error Types in WordPress

Before diving into the diagnostic process, it's crucial to understand the various error types prevalent in WordPress. These errors can manifest as PHP errors, database errors, HTTP errors, or even specific plugin and theme-related issues. PHP errors may include syntax errors, undefined function errors, or fatal errors that halt script execution. Database errors can arise from connection issues, SQL syntax errors, or database corruption. HTTP errors, such as "404 Not Found" or "500 Internal Server Error," can occur due to misconfigurations or server-related problems. Plugin and theme-related issues may lead to conflicts that affect website functionality. By recognizing these distinct error types, you'll be better prepared to target your diagnostic efforts and efficiently resolve issues.

Solution:
For PHP errors, carefully review the error messages to identify

the exact problem areas in your code. Locate and rectify syntax errors, ensure all required functions are defined and properly called, and address any fatal errors by checking the corresponding code or plugin. For database errors, check the database connection credentials and configuration. Analyze error logs to identify SQL syntax errors and address them accordingly. If a database corruption issue is suspected, consider restoring from a recent backup. For HTTP errors, inspect server configurations, plugin settings, or theme files to pinpoint the cause. Resolve conflicts between plugins and themes by deactivating or updating conflicting components.

Analyzing Error Logs

Error logs are invaluable allies in diagnosing WordPress errors, providing a detailed record of events and occurrences within your website's ecosystem. PHP error logs record script errors, warnings, and notices, while database logs capture database-related events. Understanding how to access and interpret error logs is crucial for identifying the occurrence of errors and uncovering potential issues.

Solution:
To access PHP error logs, enable WordPress debugging mode by modifying the `wp-config.php` file. Navigate to the "wp-content" directory to find the "debug.log" file, which contains PHP error logs. Use the information from the log to identify specific errors and their timestamps. For database errors, check the database server's error logs or use a plugin that records database queries and errors. Analyze database logs to uncover connection issues, SQL errors, or potential database corruption.

Debugging Techniques

Debugging serves as a powerful tool in the diagnostic process, allowing you to explore the inner workings of your WordPress website and identify problematic areas. We introduce different debugging techniques and methodologies, such as enabling WordPress debugging mode, using debug plugins, and leveraging browser developer tools. These techniques equip you with the ability to step through code, inspect variables, and trace the execution flow, uncovering the root causes behind errors in a systematic manner.

Solution:
Enable WordPress debugging mode by adding `define('WP_DEBUG', true);` to your `wp-config.php` file. This enables WordPress to display PHP errors on the front end and write them to the "debug.log" file. Use a debug plugin like "Query Monitor" or "Debug Bar" to gain insights into database queries, PHP errors, and performance metrics. Leverage browser developer tools, such as Chrome DevTools or Firefox Developer Tools, to inspect front-end issues, view console messages, and debug JavaScript errors.

Troubleshooting PHP Errors
PHP errors are common occurrences in WordPress websites and can range from syntax errors to fatal errors that cause your site to crash. We provide insights into diagnosing and resolving these PHP errors, guiding you through the process of understanding error messages, locating faulty code, and fixing the issues. Armed with this knowledge, you'll be able to navigate PHP-related challenges and optimize your website's code for enhanced performance.

Solution:
For syntax errors, carefully review the code and check for missing semicolons, parentheses, or brackets. Use code editors with syntax highlighting and error highlighting to identify and fix syntax errors promptly. For fatal errors, locate the code causing the issue and fix the problematic sections. You can comment out or remove the faulty code or deactivate the corresponding plugin or theme temporarily to identify the source of the error.

Addressing Database Errors

Database connectivity issues can lead to a myriad of problems, from broken functionalities to incomplete data storage. In this section, we explore common database-related errors and the steps required to diagnose and resolve them. Understanding how to identify and rectify issues related to database connections, SQL syntax errors, and database corruption is fundamental in maintaining a stable and fully operational website.

Solution:
For database connection issues, verify the accuracy of database credentials in your `wp-config.php` file. Ensure the correct database host, username, password, and database name are specified. If necessary, contact your hosting provider for the correct credentials. For SQL syntax errors, carefully review the problematic SQL query and fix any syntax mistakes. Use prepared statements and sanitize user inputs to prevent SQL injection attacks. For database corruption, consider restoring from a recent backup or using database repair tools and plugins to fix corrupted tables.

Resolving HTTP Errors
HTTP errors manifest as response codes that communicate specific issues between the web server and the browser. We delve into common HTTP errors, such as the notorious "404 Not Found," the "500 Internal Server Error," and the "503 Service Unavailable." These errors can result from misconfigurations, server issues, or conflicts between plugins or themes. Understanding how to diagnose and resolve HTTP errors is essential for maintaining a smooth user experience on your website.

Solution:
For "404 Not Found" errors, check your website's permalinks settings to ensure they are correct. Regenerate your website's rewrite rules by navigating to the Permalinks settings and clicking "Save Changes." If the error persists, inspect

your .htaccess file for potential issues or deactivate conflicting plugins. For "500 Internal Server Error," check your server's error logs to identify the specific cause. It may be due to PHP issues, faulty server configurations, or exhausted server resources. Resolve these issues accordingly, such as increasing PHP memory limits or fixing .htaccess rules. For "503 Service Unavailable," it could be a temporary issue caused by high server load or server maintenance. Wait for a few minutes and try accessing your website again. If the error persists, contact your hosting provider for assistance.

Error Troubleshooting Workflow
To optimize your diagnostic efforts, we present a structured error troubleshooting workflow. This systematic approach guides you through the step-by-step process of identifying, diagnosing, and resolving WordPress errors efficiently. By following this workflow, you'll be able to streamline your troubleshooting process, minimize downtime, and provide seamless user experiences to your website visitors.

Solution:
1. *Identify the Error*: Begin by recognizing the symptoms of the error and categorizing the error type (PHP, database, HTTP, etc.).
2. *Enable Debugging*: Enable WordPress debugging mode and inspect error logs to gain insights into the specific errors occurring on your website.
3. *Isolate the Problem*: Temporarily deactivate plugins and switch to a default theme to determine if the issue is caused by conflicts.
4. *Analyze Error Messages*: Analyze error messages to identify the source of the error and the affected components.
5. *Check Code and Configuration*: Inspect code files and configurations related to the error to locate and fix the problem.

6. ***Perform Database Checks***: Verify the database connection, diagnose SQL syntax errors, and repair corrupted database tables if necessary.
7. ***Optimize Performance***: Optimize your website's performance by cleaning up redundant data, optimizing database tables, and implementing caching solutions.
8. ***Update Components***: Ensure that your WordPress core, themes, and plugins are up to date to prevent known issues and vulnerabilities.
9. ***Seek Community Support***: If you encounter persistent issues, seek help from the WordPress community and support forums for insights and potential solutions.

In conclusion, this chapter equips you with the indispensable skill of diagnosing WordPress errors. Through an in-depth understanding of error types, error logs, debugging techniques, and specific error resolution strategies, you'll possess the toolkit required to tackle a wide range of common website issues. Diagnosing errors marks a pivotal step in the troubleshooting journey, allowing you to wield your knowledge and expertise to restore your WordPress website to optimal functionality and maintain a seamless user experience. As you continue your WordPress troubleshooting journey, the knowledge gained from this chapter will serve as a valuable resource to overcome challenges and ensure your WordPress website operates at its best.

CHAPTER 4: DEBUGGING TECHNIQUES AND TOOLS

In this essential chapter, we delve deep into the world of debugging techniques and tools—a crucial aspect of the WordPress troubleshooting process. Debugging is the art of identifying and fixing issues within your website's code, empowering you to resolve errors and optimize your website's performance. By honing your debugging skills and leveraging powerful tools, you'll be well-equipped to tackle a wide range of common website issues and ensure a seamless user experience.

Understanding the Debugging Process
Before delving into specific techniques and tools, we lay the groundwork by discussing the fundamentals of the debugging process. We explore the importance of systematic and methodical approaches to debugging, emphasizing the significance of taking a step-by-step and targeted approach. Understanding the debugging process enables you to navigate through complex codebases with confidence, effectively pinpointing problem areas and identifying potential solutions.

Solution:

1. *Start with a Reproducible Case*: Begin debugging by replicating the issue in a controlled environment. Isolate the conditions that trigger the problem to narrow down the scope of your investigation.
2. *Divide and Conquer*: Divide the codebase into smaller sections to pinpoint the location of the error. Temporarily comment out or deactivate portions of

the code to identify the problematic section.

3. *Use Print Statements*: Insert print statements or log entries at strategic points in your code to output variable values and the execution flow. This helps you understand how the code behaves during runtime.

4. *Analyze Error Messages*: Pay close attention to error messages or warning notices, as they often provide valuable clues about the root cause of the issue.

5. *Step Through the Code*: Utilize step-by-step debugging techniques to traverse through your code, line by line. Observe variable values and control flow to identify discrepancies and unexpected behaviors.

Enabling WordPress Debugging Mode

WordPress offers a built-in debugging mode that provides valuable insights into code errors, warnings, and notices. We walk you through the process of enabling and utilizing this feature, allowing you to access detailed error messages and logs directly from your website. By leveraging WordPress debugging mode, you'll gain a clearer understanding of issues occurring within your site's PHP code and uncover potential causes of malfunctions.

Solution:

1. *Edit the wp-config.php File*: Open your website's "wp-config.php" file using a code editor.

2. *Enable Debugging*: Add the following line of code to the file: define('WP_DEBUG', true); This enables WordPress debugging mode.

3. *Specify Error Display*: Optionally, you can add the following line to display errors on the front end: define('WP_DEBUG_DISPLAY', true);

4. *Log Errors*: To log errors to a file, add the following line: define('WP_DEBUG_LOG', true); This creates a "debug.log" file in the "wp-content" directory, recording errors and warnings.

Debugging Plugins and Themes

Plugins and themes play a pivotal role in WordPress websites, and issues arising from their interactions are common. We explore techniques for debugging plugins and themes, helping you identify conflicts, isolate problematic code, and resolve compatibility issues. By understanding how to conduct plugin and theme-specific debugging, you'll be able to unleash the full potential of these valuable extensions while maintaining a stable website environment.

Solution:

1. *Deactivate Conflicting Plugins/Themes*: If you suspect a plugin or theme conflict, start by deactivating all non-essential plugins or switching to a default theme. Then, reactivate them one by one to identify the culprit.

2. *Use Debug Plugins*: Leverage debugging plugins like "Query Monitor" or "Debug Bar" to gain insights into database queries, PHP errors, and performance metrics. These plugins provide valuable information about the state of your website during runtime.

3. *Review Code and Templates*: Analyze the code of conflicting plugins or themes to identify potential issues. Look for syntax errors, incorrect function calls, or outdated code that may cause conflicts.

4. *Check Browser Console*: Use browser developer tools to inspect and debug front-end issues. The browser console can display JavaScript errors, missing assets, or issues with CSS styles.

Browser Developer Tools

Modern web browsers provide powerful developer tools that facilitate real-time inspection and debugging of web pages. We introduce you to popular browser developer tools, such as Chrome DevTools and Firefox Developer Tools, and demonstrate how to leverage these tools to inspect and manipulate HTML,

CSS, and JavaScript. By mastering browser developer tools, you'll have a comprehensive view of your website's front-end and be able to identify and fix display and functionality issues efficiently.

Solution:

1. **Open Developer Tools**: Access the browser developer tools by right-clicking on your webpage and selecting "Inspect" or pressing F12 on Windows or Command +Option+I on macOS.
2. **Inspect Elements**: Use the Element Inspector to select and inspect HTML elements, their properties, and CSS styles. Modify styles in real-time to see the effects instantly.
3. **Debug JavaScript**: Utilize the JavaScript Console to debug JavaScript code, view errors, and log messages for troubleshooting front-end functionality.
4. **Network Analysis**: Analyze network requests and responses in the Network tab of the developer tools. This allows you to identify any failed requests, slow-loading assets, or missing resources that could be causing issues.
5. **Device Emulation**: Use the Device Emulation feature to view your website's responsiveness on different devices and screen sizes. This helps you identify and fix layout and design issues specific to certain devices.

Remote Debugging with Xdebug

Xdebug is a powerful PHP extension that enables remote debugging of PHP code. We introduce you to Xdebug and demonstrate how to set it up for remote debugging. By using Xdebug, you can step through your PHP code, inspect variables, and track the flow of execution remotely, even on a live server. This invaluable tool empowers you to identify and resolve complex PHP-related issues with ease.

Solution:

1. *Install Xdebug*: Install the Xdebug extension for PHP on your server or development environment. Check the Xdebug website for the appropriate installation instructions based on your PHP version.
2. *Configure Xdebug*: Edit your PHP configuration file (php.ini) to enable Xdebug and specify the remote debugging settings. Set the `xdebug.remote_enable` and `xdebug.remote_host` parameters to allow remote debugging.
3. *Set Up IDE Integration*: Configure your Integrated Development Environment (IDE) to work with Xdebug. Popular IDEs like PhpStorm, Visual Studio Code, and NetBeans have built-in support for Xdebug.
4. *Start Debugging*: Trigger the Xdebug debugger by adding `?XDEBUG_SESSION_START=1` to the end of the URL you want to debug. This activates Xdebug and connects it to your IDE.
5. *Set Breakpoints and Inspect Variables*: Set breakpoints in your code to pause execution at specific points. Inspect variables, step through code, and analyze the flow of execution to identify and fix issues.

Leveraging Error Handling and Logging

Error handling and logging are essential techniques for capturing and recording errors and events within your WordPress website. We explore how to implement error handling mechanisms, such as try-catch blocks, custom error handlers, and logging libraries. By leveraging error handling and logging, you'll be able to identify, record, and respond to errors and unexpected behavior more efficiently.

Solution:

1. *Implement try-catch Blocks*: Use try-catch blocks in your PHP code to catch and handle exceptions gracefully. This prevents fatal errors from halting script execution and allows you to control how errors

are handled.

2. ***Create Custom Error Handlers***: Set up custom error handlers using the `set_error_handler` and `set_exception_handler` functions. These handlers give you more control over error reporting and can log or display errors in a specific format.

3. ***Use Logging Libraries***: Utilize logging libraries like Monolog to record errors, warnings, and other events to log files. Log files provide a comprehensive record of activities and errors that occur during the execution of your website.

4. ***Monitor Error Logs***: Regularly review your error logs to identify recurring issues or emerging patterns. This helps you proactively address potential problems and optimize your website's performance.

Conclusion:

In conclusion, this chapter equips you with an arsenal of debugging techniques and tools essential for resolving common website issues. By understanding the debugging process, enabling WordPress debugging mode, debugging plugins and themes, leveraging browser developer tools, using Xdebug for remote debugging, and implementing error handling and logging mechanisms, you'll be well-prepared to tackle complex challenges within your WordPress website. Debugging is a vital skill that empowers you to identify, diagnose, and resolve issues effectively, ensuring a seamless user experience and maintaining a stable and fully functional WordPress website. As you continue your WordPress troubleshooting journey, the knowledge gained from this chapter will serve as a valuable resource to overcome obstacles and optimize your website's performance.

CHAPTER 5: TROUBLESHOOTING THEME COMPATIBILITY

In this pivotal chapter, we explore the complexities of troubleshooting theme compatibility—a common challenge faced by WordPress website owners. Themes play a crucial role in determining the appearance and layout of your website. However, conflicts between themes and other components, such as plugins or WordPress updates, can lead to unexpected issues that affect your website's functionality and aesthetics. By mastering the art of troubleshooting theme compatibility, you'll be equipped to maintain a harmonious and fully functional website, ensuring a seamless user experience.

Identifying Theme Compatibility Issues
Before delving into solutions, it's essential to recognize the signs of theme compatibility issues. These issues can manifest as layout discrepancies, missing styles, broken features, or even conflicts with plugins. By understanding the symptoms of theme compatibility problems, you can initiate targeted troubleshooting efforts and address issues promptly.

Solution:
1. ***Review Front-end and Back-end***: Carefully inspect both the front-end and back-end of your website after activating the theme. Look for any layout or style inconsistencies, broken functionalities, or error messages.

2. *Check Plugin Interactions*: Pay close attention to the behavior of installed plugins when the theme is active. Test key features and interactions to identify potential conflicts.

3. *Test Across Devices and Browsers*: Verify the theme's compatibility across various devices and web browsers. Different devices and browsers may display your website differently, highlighting compatibility issues.

Ensuring Theme and WordPress Compatibility

WordPress frequently releases updates, and theme developers often update their themes to remain compatible with the latest version. We explore techniques to ensure the theme's compatibility with the current version of WordPress, helping you avoid conflicts and security vulnerabilities.

Solution:

1. *Update WordPress and Themes*: Always keep your WordPress installation and themes up to date. This ensures you have the latest features, bug fixes, and compatibility improvements.

2. *Review Theme Changelogs*: Before updating a theme, review the theme's changelog to see if it includes compatibility updates for recent WordPress versions. This information provides insights into the changes made in each update.

3. *Test in Staging Environment*: Before applying theme updates on your live site, create a staging environment to test the updates without affecting your main website. This allows you to verify compatibility and resolve any issues before making changes on your live site.

Diagnosing Theme Conflicts with Plugins

Theme conflicts with plugins are common occurrences that can result in broken features or erratic behavior. We discuss techniques to diagnose theme conflicts with plugins, allowing you to isolate the problematic components and resolve compatibility issues.

Solution:

1. ***Disable Plugins***: Temporarily deactivate all plugins and test your website's functionality with the theme. If the issues disappear, reactivate the plugins one by one to identify the conflicting plugin.
2. ***Test with Default Theme***: Switch to a default WordPress theme, such as Twenty Twenty-One, and assess whether the issues persist. If not, it indicates a theme-specific conflict.
3. ***Check Plugin and Theme Updates***: Ensure both the plugin and theme are up to date, as outdated versions can cause compatibility issues. If a conflict arises, check if either the plugin or theme has released a recent update to address the conflict.

Resolving Theme and Plugin Styles Conflicts

Conflicts between theme and plugin styles can lead to visual discrepancies and layout issues on your website. We delve into techniques to resolve these conflicts, restoring a consistent and visually appealing user experience.

Solution:

1. ***Use Theme-specific Hooks***: Many plugins offer theme-specific hooks or filters that allow you to customize the plugin's appearance within your theme. Utilize these hooks to modify the styles and ensure a seamless integration.
2. ***Use Custom CSS***: Add custom CSS code to override conflicting styles and align the plugin's appearance with your theme. Use browser developer tools to inspect and identify the CSS classes and properties causing conflicts.
3. ***Seek Plugin Support***: If the plugin and theme conflicts

persist, reach out to the plugin's support team for guidance. They may offer specific solutions or custom CSS code to resolve compatibility issues.

Handling Theme Customization Issues

Theme customization issues can arise when customizing your theme using the WordPress Customizer or theme options. We provide strategies to troubleshoot these issues and ensure that your customizations are preserved without causing conflicts.

Solution:

1. *Review Customization Settings*: Check the theme's customization settings to ensure that they are correctly configured. Incorrect settings may lead to unexpected behavior or conflicts with other components.
2. *Use Child Themes*: If you plan to make extensive customizations to your theme, consider using a child theme. Child themes allow you to preserve your changes even after theme updates, reducing the risk of compatibility issues.
3. *Test Customizations on Staging*: Before applying significant customizations on your live site, test them on a staging environment to verify compatibility and identify potential conflicts.

Seeking Theme Support and Documentation

Theme developers often provide extensive support and documentation to address user queries and troubleshoot issues. We discuss the importance of leveraging theme support and documentation as valuable resources for resolving compatibility problems.

Solution:

1. *Consult Theme Documentation*: Thoroughly review the theme's documentation to gain insights into proper setup, customization options, and potential conflicts.

2. ***Reach Out to Theme Support***: If you encounter compatibility issues that you cannot resolve on your own, contact the theme's support team for assistance. They can offer specific solutions and recommendations for your website's unique setup.

3. ***Community Forums and Discussions***: Participate in theme-related community forums and discussions to seek help from experienced users who may have encountered similar compatibility challenges.

Conclusion:

In conclusion, this chapter equips you with the expertise to troubleshoot theme compatibility issues effectively. By identifying compatibility problems, ensuring theme and WordPress compatibility, diagnosing theme conflicts with plugins, resolving style conflicts, handling theme customization issues, and leveraging theme support and documentation, you'll be well-prepared to maintain a harmonious and visually appealing website. Theme compatibility is essential for providing a seamless user experience, and the insights gained from this chapter will empower you to address compatibility challenges proactively and ensure your WordPress website operates at its best. As you continue your WordPress troubleshooting journey, the knowledge from this chapter will serve as a valuable resource to overcome theme-related obstacles and maintain a website that captivates and engages your audience.

CHAPTER 6: FIXING PLUGIN CONFLICTS

In this critical chapter, we delve into the intricacies of fixing plugin conflicts—a prevalent challenge faced by WordPress website owners. Plugins greatly enhance the functionality of your website, but conflicts between plugins can lead to unexpected errors, broken features, or even site crashes. By mastering the art of fixing plugin conflicts, you'll be empowered to maintain a stable and fully functional website, ensuring a smooth user experience and maximizing the potential of your chosen plugins.

Identifying Plugin Conflicts
Before diving into solutions, it's essential to recognize the signs of plugin conflicts. These conflicts can manifest as broken functionalities, error messages, or unresponsive pages. Identifying plugin conflicts early on allows you to pinpoint problematic plugins and implement effective solutions promptly.

Solution:
1. ***Review Recently Installed Plugins***: If you encounter issues after installing a new plugin, it's a strong indicator of a potential conflict. Review the list of recently installed plugins to identify the one causing the problem.
2. ***Check Error Messages***: Pay close attention to error messages displayed on your website. Error messages often include the name of the plugin responsible for

the issue.

3. *Test Plugins Individually*: Disable all plugins and reactivate them one by one while checking for issues. This process helps you identify the specific plugin causing conflicts.

Update and Verify Plugin Compatibility

Plugin developers frequently release updates to improve functionality and address compatibility issues. We explore techniques to ensure that your plugins are up-to-date and compatible with your WordPress version.

Solution:

1. *Update WordPress and Plugins*: Keep your WordPress installation and all installed plugins up to date. Regular updates help resolve known issues and enhance overall performance.

2. *Check Plugin Changelogs*: Review the changelogs of each plugin to see if compatibility updates have been included for recent WordPress versions. This information provides insights into the changes made in each update.

3. *Test in Staging Environment*: Before applying plugin updates on your live site, create a staging environment to test the updates without affecting your main website. This allows you to verify compatibility and resolve any conflicts before making changes on your live site.

Isolate the Conflicting Plugins

Isolating conflicting plugins is a crucial step in fixing plugin conflicts. We provide strategies to identify the conflicting plugins and resolve the issue.

Solution:

1. *Disable All Plugins*: Temporarily disable all plugins and verify if the issue persists. If the problem disappears, it

indicates a plugin conflict.

2. *Re-enable Plugins Individually*: Re-enable plugins one by one while testing for the issue after each activation. This process helps you identify the specific plugin causing the conflict.

3. *Identify Theme-specific Conflicts*: Some plugins may conflict with specific themes. If the issue is theme-related, check the plugin's documentation or support forum for theme compatibility recommendations.

Use Plugin Compatibility Tools and Utilities

There are various tools and utilities available to assist in diagnosing and fixing plugin conflicts. We explore these resources to streamline your troubleshooting efforts.

Solution:

1. *Plugin Compatibility Checkers*: Some plugins and online tools can check the compatibility of installed plugins with your WordPress version. Use these tools to identify potentially incompatible plugins.

2. *Plugin Conflict Testers*: Specialized plugins can help you test for conflicts between active plugins. These plugins simulate conflicts and display any issues encountered during the test.

3. *Error Log Analysis*: Analyze your website's error logs to identify specific errors caused by plugins. Error logs often pinpoint the plugin responsible for the conflict.

Update or Replace Conflicting Plugins

Once you've identified the conflicting plugins, it's time to take action and resolve the issue. We discuss strategies to update or replace the conflicting plugins to restore full functionality to your website.

Solution:

1. *Update Conflicting Plugins*: Check if the conflicting plugins have newer versions that address

compatibility issues. Update the plugins to the latest version to resolve the conflict.

2. **Seek Plugin Support**: If the plugin conflict persists, reach out to the plugin's support team for assistance. They can offer specific solutions or custom patches to resolve compatibility issues.

3. **Replace Incompatible Plugins**: If a plugin is no longer maintained or lacks compatibility updates, consider replacing it with an alternative plugin that provides similar functionality without causing conflicts.

Use Plugin Compatibility Patches

In some cases, plugin conflicts can be resolved using compatibility patches. We explore techniques to create or obtain patches that address specific conflicts.

Solution:

1. **Consult Plugin Documentation**: Check the plugin's documentation or support forum for any known conflicts and available patches. Plugin developers may provide guidance on resolving compatibility issues.

2. **Create Custom Compatibility Patches**: If you have coding skills, you can create custom patches to resolve conflicts between plugins. These patches should target specific conflicts and ensure smooth coexistence.

3. **Seek Community Contributions**: Some plugin communities offer compatibility patches created by other users. Check community forums or GitHub repositories for patches that address common conflicts.

Conclusion:

In conclusion, this chapter equips you with the expertise to fix plugin conflicts effectively. By identifying conflicts, ensuring plugin compatibility, isolating problematic plugins, using compatibility tools and utilities, updating or replacing conflicting plugins, and leveraging compatibility patches, you'll be well-prepared to maintain a fully functional WordPress website. Plugin conflicts are common occurrences, but with the insights gained from this chapter, you'll be able to approach them with confidence and maintain a harmonious plugin ecosystem. As you continue your WordPress troubleshooting journey, the knowledge from this chapter will serve as a valuable resource to overcome plugin-related obstacles and optimize your website's performance.

CHAPTER 7: RESOLVING DATABASE CONNECTION PROBLEMS

In this crucial chapter, we delve into the intricacies of resolving database connection problems—an issue that can significantly impact the functionality and performance of your WordPress website. The database serves as the backbone of your website, storing critical data such as posts, pages, settings, and user information. When database connection issues arise, it can lead to errors, missing content, or even render your website inaccessible. By mastering the art of resolving database connection problems, you'll be empowered to maintain a stable and fully operational website, ensuring a seamless user experience.

Understanding Database Connection Errors
Before exploring solutions, it's essential to understand the nature of database connection errors. These errors can be caused by incorrect database credentials, server issues, or even corrupted database files. Recognizing the symptoms of database connection problems allows you to initiate targeted troubleshooting efforts.

Solution:
1. *Review Error Messages*: Pay close attention to error messages displayed on your website or in your web server logs. Common error messages include "Error establishing a database connection" or database-

related error codes.

2. ***Check wp-config.php***: Review the wp-config.php file in your WordPress root directory to ensure that the database credentials are accurate. Incorrect values for database name, username, password, or host can lead to connection errors.

3. ***Test Database Connectivity***: Use database management tools or PHP scripts to test the connection to your database server. This helps you verify whether the issue lies with the server or the WordPress configuration.

Verifying Database Server Availability

A common cause of database connection problems is the unavailability of the database server. Server downtime or maintenance can disrupt database access and render your website inaccessible.

Solution:

1. ***Contact Your Hosting Provider***: If you suspect the database server is down, contact your hosting provider to inquire about any server outages or scheduled maintenance. They can provide valuable insights into server status.

2. **Monitor Server Status**: Utilize server monitoring tools or services to track the availability and performance of your database server. This proactive approach helps you identify potential issues early on.

3. **Check Server Resources**: Insufficient server resources, such as CPU or memory, can affect the database server's performance. Review server resource utilization to ensure it meets your website's requirements.

Fixing Database Connection Credentials

Incorrect or outdated database credentials can lead to database connection errors. We explore techniques to fix database connection credentials and restore database access.

Solution:

1. ***Verify Database Credentials***: Double-check the database name, username, password, and host specified in the wp-config.php file. Ensure they match the credentials provided by your hosting provider.
2. ***Reset Database Password***: If you suspect an incorrect password, reset the database user's password through your hosting control panel or database management tool.
3. ***Update wp-config.php***: If you've recently changed database credentials, ensure that the new credentials are updated in the wp-config.php file. Incorrect credentials will lead to connection errors.

Addressing SQL Syntax Errors

SQL syntax errors in your database queries can cause connection problems and affect your website's functionality. We explore techniques to identify and resolve SQL syntax errors.

Solution:

1. ***Review Recent Changes***: If the database connection issue coincides with recent changes, review the code or plugin that made the changes. Check for any SQL queries with syntax errors.
2. ***Use Prepared Statements***: Implement prepared statements or query escaping functions in your database queries to prevent SQL injection attacks and avoid syntax errors caused by improper data handling.
3. ***Check Plugin and Theme Functions***: Examine custom database queries in your theme or plugin files for syntax errors. Use debugging techniques to trace the execution flow and identify problematic queries.

Fixing Database Corruption Issues

Database corruption can lead to severe connection problems and data loss. It's essential to address database corruption promptly to ensure the integrity of your website's data.

<u>Solution</u>:
1. **Use Database Repair Tools**: WordPress includes built-in database repair functionality. Add the following line to your wp-config.php file to enable it: define('WP_ALLOW_REPAIR', true); Visit the "wp-admin/maint/repair.php" URL to access the repair tool and follow the on-screen instructions.
2. **Restore from Backup**: If you have a recent database backup, consider restoring the database from that backup. Restoring from a clean backup can resolve corruption issues.
3. **Seek Professional Assistance**: If you're unsure about the extent of the database corruption or are uncomfortable performing repair operations, seek help from a professional database administrator or your hosting provider.

Optimizing Database Performance

Optimizing your database performance can prevent connection problems and enhance your website's speed and responsiveness. We explore techniques to optimize your database.

<u>Solution</u>:
1. **Optimize Database Tables**: Use database optimization plugins or built-in tools to clean up and optimize database tables. This reduces the size of the database and improves query performance.
2. **Reduce Database Queries**: Minimize the number of database queries executed on each page load. Use caching plugins and techniques to serve cached pages and reduce the need for frequent database access.
3. **Use a Content Delivery Network (CDN)**: Offload static assets and media files to a CDN, reducing the load on your database server and improving overall site

performance.

Conclusion:

In conclusion, this chapter equips you with the expertise to resolve database connection problems effectively. By understanding database connection errors, verifying database server availability, fixing database connection credentials, addressing SQL syntax errors, fixing database corruption issues, and optimizing database performance, you'll be well-prepared to maintain a fully functional and stable WordPress website. The database serves as the backbone of your website, and the insights gained from this chapter will empower you to handle database-related challenges proactively and ensure your WordPress website operates at its best. As you continue your WordPress troubleshooting journey, the knowledge from this chapter will serve as a valuable resource to overcome database connection issues and optimize your website's performance.

CHAPTER 8: SOLVING WORDPRESS WHITE SCREEN OF DEATH

In this critical chapter, we tackle one of the most daunting issues faced by WordPress website owners—the White Screen of Death (WSOD). This frustrating problem occurs when your website displays a blank, white screen instead of its usual content. The WSOD can be caused by a variety of factors, including plugin conflicts, theme issues, PHP errors, or exhausted server resources. By mastering the art of solving the WordPress White Screen of Death, you'll be empowered to quickly restore your website's functionality and provide a seamless user experience.

Understanding the White Screen of Death
Before exploring solutions, it's essential to understand the nature of the White Screen of Death and its potential causes. The WSOD can manifest on both the front-end and back-end of your website, making it challenging to pinpoint the exact issue.

Solution:

1. *Review Error Logs*: Access your website's error logs via your hosting provider or the server's file system. Error logs often provide insights into the specific errors or warnings triggering the WSOD.

2. *Check Front-end and Back-end*: Verify whether the WSOD occurs on the front-end of your website, visible to visitors, or the back-end, affecting your WordPress admin dashboard.

3. *Isolate Recent Changes*: If the WSOD coincides with recent changes to your website, such as plugin installations or updates, it may indicate a conflict or compatibility issue.

Diagnosing Plugin and Theme Conflicts

Plugin and theme conflicts are common culprits behind the White Screen of Death. We explore techniques to diagnose and resolve these conflicts to restore your website's functionality.

Solution:

1. *Disable All Plugins*: Temporarily disable all plugins to check if the WSOD persists. If the issue disappears, it indicates a plugin conflict.
2. *Test with Default Theme*: Switch to a default WordPress theme, such as Twenty Twenty-One, to determine if the WSOD is theme-related. If the issue is resolved with the default theme, it points to a theme-specific conflict.
3. *Re-enable Plugins and Themes*: Reactivate plugins and themes one by one while checking for the WSOD after each activation. This process helps you identify the specific plugin or theme causing the conflict.

Dealing with Exhausted PHP Memory

Insufficient PHP memory can trigger the White Screen of Death, especially when executing resource-intensive tasks or loading large datasets.

Solution:

1. *Increase PHP Memory Limit*: Access your website's "wp-config.php" file and add the following line of code above the "/* That's all, stop editing! */" line: define('WP_MEMORY_LIMIT', '256M'); This increases the PHP memory limit to 256MB. Adjust the value based on your website's requirements.
2. *Check Memory Limit Settings*: If your hosting

environment restricts PHP memory usage, contact your hosting provider to request a memory limit increase or consider upgrading your hosting plan.

Handling PHP Errors and Warnings

PHP errors and warnings can lead to the White Screen of Death. These errors can be related to code syntax issues, function conflicts, or compatibility problems.

Solution:

1. *Enable WordPress Debugging*: Enable WordPress debugging mode by adding the following line to your "wp-config.php" file: define('WP_DEBUG', true); This allows you to see detailed PHP error messages on your website.
2. *Inspect Error Logs*: Check your website's error logs to identify specific PHP errors and warnings. Error logs provide valuable clues to troubleshoot the issue.
3. *Check Recently Edited Files*: Review files you recently edited, such as theme files or custom code snippets. Incorrect changes may cause PHP errors and lead to the WSOD.

Repairing Core Files and Plugins

Corrupted core files or plugins can trigger the White Screen of Death. Repairing or replacing these files can help restore your website's functionality.

Solution:

1. *Reinstall WordPress Core Files*: Download a fresh copy of WordPress from wordpress.org and replace the core files on your server. This process ensures that corrupted files are replaced with clean versions.
2. *Reinstall Problematic Plugins*: For plugins suspected of causing the WSOD, deactivate and delete them from your WordPress admin dashboard. Then, reinstall the plugins from the official WordPress repository or a

trusted source.

Seek Professional Assistance

In some cases, resolving the White Screen of Death may require expert help. Complex issues or server-related problems may be best handled by professionals.

Solution:

1. *Contact WordPress Support*: Reach out to the official WordPress support forums or community for assistance. Experienced members can provide guidance and solutions based on their expertise.
2. *Consult Hosting Support*: If the WSOD is caused by server-related issues, contact your hosting provider's support team. They can investigate server configurations and provide solutions.
3. *Hire WordPress Experts*: Consider hiring experienced WordPress developers or consultants to troubleshoot and resolve persistent WSOD issues. These professionals can identify and fix complex problems effectively.

Conclusion:

In conclusion, this chapter equips you with the expertise to solve the WordPress White Screen of Death effectively. By understanding the nature of the WSOD, diagnosing plugin and theme conflicts, addressing exhausted PHP memory, handling PHP errors and warnings, repairing core files and plugins, and seeking professional assistance when necessary, you'll be well-prepared to swiftly overcome the White Screen of Death and restore your WordPress website to full functionality. The White Screen of Death can be a frustrating and alarming issue, but with the insights gained from this chapter, you'll be able to approach it with confidence and resolve the problem efficiently.

As you continue your WordPress troubleshooting journey, remember that the White Screen of Death can be caused by a variety of factors, and it's essential to approach each situation methodically. By following the troubleshooting steps outlined in this chapter and leveraging the available tools and resources, you'll be able to pinpoint the root cause of the WSOD and apply the appropriate solutions.

The White Screen of Death is a testament to the dynamic nature of WordPress and the vast array of plugins and themes available. With this understanding, you can continue to experiment with new plugins and themes, confident in your ability to diagnose and resolve any compatibility issues that may arise.

In conclusion, the insights and solutions provided in this chapter empower you to overcome the WordPress White Screen of Death and ensure the continuous and seamless operation of your website. By honing your troubleshooting skills and understanding the intricacies of the WSOD, you become better equipped to handle any future challenges that come your way. As you apply the knowledge gained from this chapter and throughout the book, you'll solidify your role as a WordPress troubleshooter, ensuring your website remains a reliable, user-friendly, and engaging platform for your audience. Happy troubleshooting!

CHAPTER 9: DEALING WITH WORDPRESS UPDATE ISSUES

In this crucial chapter, we address the challenges and solutions related to WordPress update issues. Regularly updating WordPress core, themes, and plugins is essential for security, performance, and new features. However, update problems can occur, leading to broken websites, missing content, or compatibility conflicts. By mastering the art of dealing with WordPress update issues, you'll be empowered to keep your website up-to-date and functioning smoothly.

Understanding WordPress Update Errors

Before exploring solutions, it's vital to understand the nature of WordPress update errors. These errors can manifest during core updates, theme updates, or plugin updates and may be caused by various factors.

Solution:

1. **Review Update Logs**: Access the update logs on your WordPress admin dashboard or server to identify specific errors or warnings encountered during the update process.
2. **Check Compatibility**: Verify if your installed themes and plugins are compatible with the latest WordPress version. Incompatibility can lead to update issues and conflicts.
3. **Test in Staging Environment**: Before updating on your live site, create a staging environment to test the updates. This allows you to identify and resolve

potential issues before impacting your live website.

Troubleshooting Core Update Problems

Updating the WordPress core is a fundamental aspect of website maintenance. However, core update issues can arise due to server configurations, file permissions, or plugin conflicts.

Solution:

1. *Enable Debugging*: Enable WordPress debugging mode by adding the following line to your "wp-config.php" file: define('WP_DEBUG', true); This provides more detailed error messages during the update process.
2. *Verify File Permissions*: Check file permissions on your WordPress files and folders. Ensure that the appropriate permissions are set to allow updates to occur.
3. *Disable Plugins*: Temporarily deactivate all plugins and attempt the core update again. If the update succeeds, it indicates a plugin conflict.

Resolving Theme Update Issues

Updating your WordPress theme is essential for obtaining new features and bug fixes. However, theme update problems can occur due to customization conflicts or outdated themes.

Solution:

1. *Create a Child Theme*: If you've made extensive customizations to your theme, consider creating a child theme. Child themes preserve your customizations while allowing the parent theme to be updated without conflicts.
2. *Backup and Rollback*: Before updating the theme, create a complete backup of your website. If the update causes issues, you can easily roll back to the previous version.
3. *Check Theme Changelog*: Review the theme's changelog to see if the latest update includes compatibility fixes

or specific instructions for updating.

Addressing Plugin Update Conflicts

Updating plugins is critical for maintaining security and optimal performance. However, conflicts with other plugins or outdated versions can hinder smooth updates.

Solution:

1. *Update Plugins Sequentially*: Instead of updating all plugins simultaneously, update them one by one. This allows you to identify which plugin update is causing conflicts.
2. *Check Plugin Compatibility*: Verify if the plugin is compatible with the latest WordPress version. Review the plugin's documentation or support forum for compatibility information.
3. *Seek Plugin Support*: If an update conflict persists, contact the plugin's support team for assistance. They can provide guidance or release a patch to resolve the issue.

Handling Failed Updates and Rollbacks

In some cases, updates may fail, leaving your website in an unstable state. Handling failed updates and rollbacks is crucial to restoring your website's functionality.

Solution:

1. *Restore from Backup*: If a failed update causes significant issues, restore your website from a recent backup. Backups ensure you can revert to a stable version of your site.
2. *Use Version Control*: If you use version control systems like Git, you can roll back to a previous version of your website's code to undo the update.
3. *Troubleshoot Error Messages*: Carefully read and analyze any error messages or logs generated during the update process. Error messages provide insights

into the root cause of the failed update.

Avoiding Update Problems in the Future

Prevention is the key to avoiding future update issues. We explore best practices to follow to ensure smooth and hassle-free updates.

Solution:

1. *Regular Backups*: Maintain regular backups of your website to ensure you have a restore point in case of update problems.
2. *Update Regularly*: Regularly update WordPress core, themes, and plugins to stay up-to-date with the latest features, security patches, and bug fixes.
3. *Test Updates in Staging*: Before applying updates to your live site, test them in a staging environment to identify and resolve potential conflicts or issues.

Conclusion:

In conclusion, this chapter equips you with the expertise to deal with WordPress update issues effectively. By understanding update errors, troubleshooting core, theme, and plugin update problems, addressing failed updates, and following best practices for future updates, you'll be well-prepared to maintain an updated, secure, and fully functional WordPress website. Updates are crucial for your website's performance and security, and the insights gained from this chapter will empower you to approach updates with confidence and handle any challenges that may arise. As you continue your WordPress troubleshooting journey, the knowledge from this chapter will serve as a valuable resource to keep your website running smoothly and up-to-date, providing a seamless experience for your audience. Happy updating!

CHAPTER 10: RECOVERING FROM HACKED WORDPRESS SITES

In this critical chapter, we address the distressing and unfortunate situation of dealing with hacked WordPress sites. Website security is paramount, but even with precautions, websites can still fall victim to hacking attempts. When your WordPress site gets hacked, it can lead to unauthorized access, malicious content, or a compromised user experience. By mastering the art of recovering from hacked WordPress sites, you'll be empowered to restore your website's integrity, protect user data, and prevent future security breaches.

Identifying Hacked WordPress Sites
Before exploring solutions, it's essential to recognize the signs of a hacked WordPress site. Hackers often conceal their activities, making it challenging to identify security breaches.

Solution:
1. ***Check for Unexpected Changes***: Regularly inspect your website for any unexpected changes, such as unauthorized user accounts, altered content, or new admin privileges.
2. ***Review Server and Security Logs***: Access your server logs and security logs to identify suspicious activities or unauthorized access attempts.
3. ***Use Security Plugins***: Employ security plugins that offer malware scanning and intrusion detection features to

proactively monitor your site for potential threats.

Containing the Damage

When your WordPress site is hacked, it's crucial to act swiftly to limit the damage and prevent further compromise.

Solution:

1. *Isolate the Site*: Take the website offline temporarily to prevent users from accessing the compromised content. This action gives you time to assess the situation and implement necessary security measures.
2. *Change Passwords*: Reset all user passwords, especially those with administrative privileges. Ensure that strong passwords are used for enhanced security.
3. *Close Vulnerabilities*: Identify and close security vulnerabilities that hackers may have exploited. This includes updating WordPress core, themes, and plugins to their latest versions.

Cleaning and Restoring Your Website

After containing the damage, the next step is to clean and restore your WordPress website to its original state.

Solution:

1. *Use Malware Scanners*: Utilize malware scanning tools or security plugins to identify and remove malicious code from your website's files and database.
2. *Restore from Backup*: If you have a clean and recent backup, restore your website from that backup to eliminate any traces of the hack.
3. *Check Core Files*: Manually inspect your WordPress core files to ensure they haven't been tampered with. Replace any compromised files with fresh copies from a clean WordPress installation.

Strengthening Website Security

Preventing future hacks is crucial to maintaining a secure WordPress site. Strengthening your website's security is an ongoing process.

Solution:

1. *Implement Security Plugins*: Install reputable security plugins that offer features such as firewall protection, malware scanning, and login attempt limiting.
2. *Enable Two-Factor Authentication*: Enable two-factor authentication for all user accounts to add an extra layer of security to the login process.
3. *Regularly Update Plugins and Themes*: Keep all plugins and themes up to date with the latest versions, as updates often include security patches.

Enhancing User and Administrator Awareness

Educating users and administrators about security best practices is vital to safeguarding your WordPress site.

Solution:

1. *User Training*: Educate users about common security threats, such as phishing attacks, and the importance of using strong passwords and updating their login credentials regularly.
2. *Administrator Responsibilities*: Ensure that administrators are aware of their role in maintaining website security, including monitoring for unusual activities and promptly addressing security incidents.
3. *Back Up Regularly*: Emphasize the importance of regular website backups to administrators, as backups are essential for quick recovery in case of future hacks.

Seeking Professional Assistance

In some cases, recovering from a hacked WordPress site may require expert help. Don't hesitate to seek assistance from security professionals or WordPress specialists.

Solution:

1. *Hire a Security Expert*: Engage the services of a security expert or a specialized WordPress security

team to perform a comprehensive security audit and strengthen your website's defenses.

2. ***WordPress Support Forums***: Seek guidance from the official WordPress support forums or community. Experienced members can provide valuable insights and suggestions to address specific security issues.

3. ***Report Security Breaches***: If you believe your site's security breach may have compromised user data or violated any legal regulations, report the incident to relevant authorities and take appropriate measures to protect affected users.

Conclusion:

In conclusion, this chapter equips you with the expertise to recover from hacked WordPress sites effectively. By identifying hacked sites, containing the damage, cleaning and restoring your website, strengthening security measures, enhancing user awareness, and seeking professional assistance when needed, you'll be well-prepared to overcome security breaches and maintain a secure WordPress website. Security is of paramount importance in the digital world, and the insights gained from this chapter will empower you to approach website security with vigilance and diligence. As you continue your WordPress troubleshooting journey, the knowledge from this chapter will serve as a valuable resource to protect your website and user data from potential security threats, ensuring a safe and trustworthy online presence for your audience. Happy safeguarding!

CHAPTER 11: TROUBLESHOOTING WORDPRESS SECURITY VULNERABILITIES

In this critical chapter, we address the crucial task of troubleshooting WordPress security vulnerabilities. WordPress is a popular target for hackers, and even the most secure websites may encounter security flaws. Identifying and addressing security vulnerabilities is essential to protect your website from potential attacks, data breaches, and other malicious activities. By mastering the art of troubleshooting WordPress security vulnerabilities, you'll be empowered to fortify your website's defenses and ensure a safe online presence for your audience.

Identifying WordPress Security Vulnerabilities
Before exploring solutions, it's vital to understand the nature of WordPress security vulnerabilities. Vulnerabilities can exist in the WordPress core, themes, plugins, or custom code, making your website susceptible to attacks.

Solution:
1. ***Conduct Security Audits***: Regularly perform security audits of your website to identify potential vulnerabilities. Use security plugins or seek professional assistance to assess your site's security

posture.

2. ***Monitor Security Reports***: Keep an eye on security reports and alerts from reputable security organizations and WordPress authorities. These reports often highlight newly discovered vulnerabilities and their respective fixes.

3. ***Utilize Vulnerability Databases***: Consult vulnerability databases that list known WordPress security issues and their respective fixes. Stay informed about potential vulnerabilities that may affect your website.

Addressing WordPress Core Vulnerabilities

WordPress core vulnerabilities pose significant risks to your website's security. It's crucial to promptly address any core-related security issues.

Solution:

1. ***Update WordPress Core***: Regularly update your WordPress core to the latest version. Updates often include security patches to address known vulnerabilities.

2. ***Monitor Security Channels***: Keep track of WordPress security advisories and announcements from official sources. This information will alert you to any critical core vulnerabilities and the corresponding fixes.

3. ***Apply Hotfixes***: In case an urgent security update is released, but you can't perform a complete update immediately, apply any available hotfixes or patches provided by WordPress or the security community.

Fixing Theme and Plugin Vulnerabilities

Themes and plugins are frequent targets for hackers due to their widespread usage. Addressing theme and plugin vulnerabilities is essential to protect your website from potential breaches.

Solution:

1. ***Update Themes and Plugins***: Regularly update all

installed themes and plugins to the latest versions. Developers frequently release updates that include security fixes.

2. *Monitor Developer Changelogs*: Keep track of changelogs and release notes from theme and plugin developers. These documents outline security updates and fixes in each release.

3. *Use Trusted Sources*: Obtain themes and plugins only from reputable sources such as the official WordPress repository or known premium marketplaces. Avoid downloading files from unverified websites, as they may contain malicious code.

Implementing Strong Access Control Measures

Robust access control is a critical aspect of WordPress security. Restricting access to sensitive areas of your website helps prevent unauthorized access and potential data breaches.

Solution:

1. *Use Strong Passwords*: Encourage users to use strong, unique passwords and implement a password policy that enforces password complexity.

2. *Limit Administrator Access*: Only grant administrator access to trusted users who genuinely need it. Avoid assigning admin privileges to multiple users unless necessary.

3. *Enable Two-Factor Authentication*: Implement two-factor authentication for all user accounts to add an extra layer of security to the login process.

Securing the Website Database

The WordPress database contains sensitive information and is a common target for attacks. Securing your website database is crucial for overall security.

Solution:

1. *Change Database Prefix*: During WordPress

installation, change the default database prefix to something unique to make it harder for attackers to target your database tables.

2. *Regular Backups*: Regularly back up your website database to ensure that you have a recent copy to restore in case of a security breach or data loss.

3. *Protect Database Credentials*: Safeguard your database credentials and avoid storing them in easily accessible locations, such as code files or version control systems.

Securing Your Server Environment

A secure server environment is essential for a secure WordPress website. Troubleshoot server-related security vulnerabilities to fortify your defenses.

Solution:

1. *Use Secure Hosting*: Choose a reputable and secure hosting provider that employs robust security measures, such as firewalls, intrusion detection systems, and regular security audits.

2. *Keep Server Software Updated*: Ensure that server software, including PHP, MySQL, and the operating system, is up to date with the latest security patches.

3. *Disable Directory Listings*: Disable directory listings on your server to prevent unauthorized access to sensitive files and directories.

Implementing Website Firewall and Security Plugins

Website firewalls and security plugins offer additional layers of protection against various security threats.

Solution:

1. *Install a Website Firewall*: Consider using a website firewall to filter incoming traffic and block malicious requests.

2. *Use Security Plugins*: Install reputable security plugins that offer features such as malware scanning, brute

force protection, and login attempt limiting.

3. ***Regularly Monitor and Update***: Regularly monitor and update your security plugins to ensure they provide optimal protection against new and evolving threats.

Conclusion:

In conclusion, this chapter equips you with the expertise to troubleshoot WordPress security vulnerabilities effectively. By identifying vulnerabilities, addressing WordPress core, theme, and plugin vulnerabilities, implementing strong access control measures, securing the website database, fortifying your server environment, and leveraging website firewall and security plugins, you'll be well-prepared to safeguard your WordPress website from potential security threats. Security is a continuous process, and the insights gained from this chapter will empower you to approach website security proactively and vigilantly. As you continue your WordPress troubleshooting journey, the knowledge from this chapter will serve as a valuable resource to maintain a secure and trustworthy online presence for your audience. Happy securing!

CHAPTER 12: ADDRESSING SLOW WEBSITE PERFORMANCE

In this critical chapter, we delve into the common issue of slow website performance and explore the techniques to address it effectively. A slow-loading website can lead to frustrated visitors, higher bounce rates, and lower search engine rankings. By mastering the art of addressing slow website performance, you'll be empowered to enhance your website's speed and responsiveness, providing a seamless user experience.

Identifying the Causes of Slow Website Performance
Before exploring solutions, it's essential to understand the factors contributing to slow website performance. Various factors can affect your website's speed, including server configuration, large media files, unoptimized code, and external resources.

Solution:
1. *Use Website Speed Testing Tools*: Utilize website speed testing tools like Google PageSpeed Insights or GTmetrix to analyze your website's performance and identify potential issues.
2. *Review Server Performance*: Evaluate your hosting provider's server performance and ensure it meets your website's requirements. Consider upgrading to a better hosting plan or a managed hosting service if needed.

3. *Monitor External Resources*: Keep an eye on third-party resources like external scripts, fonts, or APIs that your website relies on. These resources can introduce delays if not optimized.

Optimizing Images and Media Files

Large and unoptimized images and media files can significantly impact website performance, causing slow load times.

Solution:

1. *Compress Images*: Use image compression tools or plugins to reduce the file size of images without compromising quality. Smaller image files load faster, improving website speed.
2. *Choose the Right Format*: Use appropriate image formats like JPEG for photographs and PNG for graphics. Each format has its strengths in terms of compression and quality.
3. *Lazy Loading*: Implement lazy loading for images and media files, ensuring they load only when they become visible to the user, reducing initial page load times.

Caching and Content Delivery Network (CDN)

Leveraging caching and a Content Delivery Network (CDN) can significantly improve your website's performance.

Solution:

1. *Use Caching Plugins*: Install caching plugins to create static versions of your website's pages. Cached pages load faster for subsequent visitors, reducing server load.
2. *Enable Browser Caching*: Set up browser caching to instruct user browsers to store static files locally, reducing the need for repeated downloads.
3. *Use a CDN*: Utilize a Content Delivery Network to distribute your website's static assets across multiple servers globally, reducing latency and speeding up

content delivery.

Minimizing HTTP Requests and Server Load

Excessive HTTP requests and server load can slow down your website's performance.

Solution:

1. *Minimize HTTP Requests*: Reduce the number of HTTP requests by combining CSS and JavaScript files, using CSS sprites, and optimizing web fonts.
2. *Optimize Code*: Optimize your website's code to reduce its size and complexity. Remove unnecessary scripts, comments, and whitespace to improve load times.
3. *Use Asynchronous Loading*: Implement asynchronous loading for non-essential scripts, allowing them to load in the background without blocking the page's rendering.

Troubleshooting Database Performance

Database queries and performance can impact your website's speed and responsiveness.

Solution:

1. *Optimize Database Queries*: Use database optimization plugins or techniques to optimize your database queries and reduce the time taken to retrieve data.
2. *Limit Post Revisions*: Control the number of post revisions stored in your database to prevent unnecessary data bloat.
3. *Regular Database Maintenance*: Perform regular database maintenance, including cleaning up unnecessary data and optimizing database tables.

Addressing Theme and Plugin Performance

Theme and plugin performance can significantly affect your website's speed and load times.

Solution:

1. ***Use Lightweight Themes***: Choose lightweight and well-coded themes that prioritize speed and performance over unnecessary features.
2. ***Limit Plugins***: Be mindful of the number of plugins you install, as each plugin introduces additional scripts and resources that can slow down your website.
3. ***Update Themes and Plugins***: Keep your themes and plugins up to date with the latest versions, as updates often include performance improvements.

Testing and Monitoring Performance
Regularly testing and monitoring your website's performance allows you to identify and address potential issues proactively.

Solution:

1. ***Regular Speed Tests***: Conduct regular speed tests to measure your website's performance and identify any declines in speed.
2. ***Monitor Website Uptime***: Use website monitoring tools to ensure your website remains available and responsive to visitors at all times.
3. ***Analyze User Behavior***: Analyze user behavior on your website to identify performance bottlenecks and areas for improvement.

Conclusion:
In conclusion, this chapter equips you with the expertise to address slow website performance effectively. By identifying the causes of slow performance, optimizing images and media files, leveraging caching and CDN, minimizing HTTP requests and server load, troubleshooting database performance, addressing theme and plugin performance, and testing and monitoring website performance, you'll be well-prepared to enhance your website's speed and provide a seamless user experience. Website speed is crucial for user satisfaction and search engine rankings, and the insights gained from this chapter will empower you to approach website performance optimization with confidence

and diligence. As you continue your WordPress troubleshooting journey, the knowledge from this chapter will serve as a valuable resource to keep your website fast, responsive, and user-friendly, ensuring a positive and engaging experience for your audience. Happy optimizing

CHAPTER 13: FIXING BROKEN LINKS AND 404 ERRORS

In this critical chapter, we address the common issue of broken links and 404 errors on WordPress websites. Broken links and 404 errors can negatively impact user experience, SEO rankings, and website credibility. By mastering the art of fixing broken links and 404 errors, you'll be empowered to provide a seamless and user-friendly browsing experience for your audience.

Identifying Broken Links and 404 Errors
Before exploring solutions, it's essential to identify broken links and 404 errors on your WordPress website. Broken links occur when the linked page no longer exists, leading to a 404 error page, indicating that the requested page cannot be found.

Solution:
1. *Use Link Checker Tools*: Utilize link checker tools or plugins to scan your website for broken links and identify the pages or posts containing these broken links.
2. *Monitor Google Search Console*: Regularly check Google Search Console for any 404 errors reported by search engines. This information provides insights into broken links that need attention.
3. *Analyze Website Analytics*: Review your website's analytics to identify the pages with high bounce rates, as this could indicate potential broken links.

Addressing Broken Links

Once you've identified broken links on your website, it's crucial to address them promptly to ensure a smooth browsing experience for visitors.

Solution:

1. ***Update Internal Links***: If the broken link is internal, ensure that the target page's URL is correct. If the target page no longer exists, consider redirecting the link to a relevant page or removing it altogether.
2. ***Fix External Links***: For broken external links, update the links to point to the correct and functioning URLs. If the external page no longer exists, consider removing the link or finding an alternative source.
3. **Use 301 Redirects**: If a page has permanently moved to a new URL, implement a 301 redirect from the old URL to the new one. This helps preserve SEO rankings and directs users to the appropriate page.

Handling 404 Errors

404 errors can frustrate visitors and negatively impact your website's SEO. It's crucial to handle them effectively to maintain a positive user experience.

Solution:

1. ***Customize 404 Page***: Create a custom 404 error page that provides helpful information, such as site navigation links or a search bar, to guide users back to relevant content.
2. ***Implement Global 404 Handling***: Utilize plugins or server configurations to implement a global 404 handling system. This ensures that any 404 errors on your website are redirected to the custom 404 page.
3. ***Regularly Monitor and Fix***: Continuously monitor your website for new 404 errors and promptly address them by updating links or implementing redirects.

Maintaining URL Structure

A consistent and well-organized URL structure helps prevent broken links and 404 errors.

Solution:
1. *Use Permalinks*: Use meaningful and SEO-friendly permalinks that reflect your content's title or topic. Avoid using generic or randomly generated URLs.
2. *Avoid Changing URLs*: Minimize URL changes for existing pages or posts, as this can lead to broken links. If URL changes are necessary, set up redirects to the new URLs.
3. *Update Internal Links*: When creating new content or restructuring your website, update internal links to reflect the updated URL structure.

Redirects and Canonicalization
Redirects and canonicalization are essential tools to prevent broken links and duplicate content issues.

Solution:
1. *Implement 301 Redirects*: Use 301 redirects for permanently moved or deleted pages to guide users and search engines to the new location.
2. *Canonical Tags*: Utilize canonical tags to indicate the preferred version of a page when dealing with duplicate content. This helps search engines index the correct version of the content.
3. *Audit and Update Redirects*: Regularly audit your website's redirects to ensure they are still valid and updated. Remove or update outdated redirects as needed.

Regular Website Maintenance
Consistent website maintenance is crucial to preventing and fixing broken links and 404 errors.

Solution:
1. *Regularly Check Links*: Routinely review your website's

links to identify and fix any broken or outdated links.

2. *Check External Links*: Monitor external links on your website to ensure they are still valid and functional. Remove or update broken external links.

3. *Perform Content Audits*: Conduct regular content audits to identify outdated or irrelevant pages and posts. Remove or update these to prevent 404 errors.

Conclusion:

In conclusion, this chapter equips you with the expertise to fix broken links and 404 errors effectively. By identifying broken links and 404 errors, addressing broken links, handling 404 errors, maintaining a proper URL structure, implementing redirects and canonicalization, and conducting regular website maintenance, you'll be well-prepared to provide a smooth and user-friendly browsing experience for your audience. Broken links and 404 errors are common challenges faced by website owners, but the insights gained from this chapter will empower you to approach these issues proactively and ensure the integrity of your website's navigation and content. As you continue your WordPress troubleshooting journey, the knowledge from this chapter will serve as a valuable resource to maintain a well-organized, error-free, and user-centric website, promoting a positive user experience and enhancing your website's overall performance. Happy fixing!

CHAPTER 14: HANDLING WORDPRESS LOGIN ISSUES

In this essential chapter, we delve into the common WordPress login issues that users may encounter and explore effective solutions to resolve them. The WordPress login is a gateway to website management, and any login-related problems can be frustrating and disruptive. By mastering the art of handling WordPress login issues, you'll be empowered to ensure smooth access for users and administrators, maintaining the security and functionality of your website.

Identifying WordPress Login Issues
Before exploring solutions, it's crucial to identify the nature of WordPress login issues. Login problems can range from forgotten passwords to server-related issues, and pinpointing the specific cause is essential for efficient troubleshooting.

Solution:

1. *Review Error Messages*: Carefully read any error messages displayed during the login process. Error messages often provide insights into the root cause of the login issue.
2. *Check Server Status*: Verify the server's status and ensure that it is online and functioning correctly. Server-related issues can affect the login process.
3. *Monitor Security Logs*: Analyze your website's security logs to identify any suspicious login attempts or potential brute force attacks.

Troubleshooting Forgotten Passwords
One of the most common login issues is users forgetting their passwords, leading to difficulties accessing their accounts.

Solution:
1. *Password Reset*: Provide a password reset option on your login page. Users can initiate a password reset by entering their email address or username.
2. *Check Spam Folder*: Advise users to check their spam or junk folders if they don't receive the password reset email promptly.
3. *WordPress Admin Email*: Ensure that the WordPress admin email is up to date, as password reset emails are sent to this address by default.

Resolving Username and Email Errors
Incorrect usernames or email addresses can prevent users from logging in successfully.

Solution:
1. *Verify Username*: Instruct users to double-check their username for typos or errors. Usernames are case-sensitive, so they must enter them correctly.
2. *Use Email Address*: If your website allows login with email addresses, users should use their correct email associated with their account.
3. *Check User Database*: Manually review your website's user database to ensure usernames and email addresses are accurately stored.

Fixing "Error Establishing a Database Connection"
The "Error Establishing a Database Connection" message can be alarming and prevent access to the WordPress login.

Solution:
1. *Check Database Credentials*: Ensure that the database credentials in the "wp-config.php" file are correct and

match those provided by your hosting provider.

2. ***Review Server Downtime***: Verify if your hosting server is experiencing downtime or connectivity issues. Contact your hosting provider if necessary.

3. ***Database Repair***: Try repairing your WordPress database using the "wp-config.php" file or plugins designed for this purpose.

Handling White Screen on the Login Page

A white screen on the login page can hinder user access and prevent administrators from logging in.

Solution:

1. ***Disable Plugins***: Temporarily deactivate all plugins via FTP or your hosting control panel to check if a plugin is causing the issue.

2. ***Clear Browser Cache***: Instruct users to clear their browser cache and cookies, as a cached login page can cause display issues.

3. ***Check Theme Compatibility***: Verify if the active theme is compatible with the current WordPress version. Switch to a default theme to check if the issue persists.

Troubleshooting Login Redirect Loop

A login redirect loop occurs when users are continuously redirected back to the login page after attempting to log in.

Solution:

1. ***Check .htaccess File***: Review your website's ".htaccess" file for any misconfigurations or redirects that might be causing the loop.

2. ***Verify Cookies Settings***: Ensure that your website's cookies settings are correctly configured to prevent login loop issues.

3. ***Reset Permalinks***: Resetting permalinks to default settings can sometimes resolve login redirect loop problems.

Resolving Server-Side Login Issues
In some cases, login issues may be related to server-side settings or restrictions.

Solution:
1. *PHP Memory Limit*: Increase the PHP memory limit in the "wp-config.php" file if it's set too low to avoid login issues.
2. *Check Server Restrictions*: Verify that your server settings are not blocking login requests or triggering security measures
3. *Contact Hosting Provider*: If the login issue persists and is related to server settings, contact your hosting provider for assistance.

Conclusion:
In conclusion, this chapter equips you with the expertise to handle WordPress login issues effectively. By identifying login problems, troubleshooting forgotten passwords, resolving username and email errors, fixing database connection errors, addressing white screen login issues, handling login redirect loops, and resolving server-side login issues, you'll be well-prepared to ensure smooth access for users and administrators to your WordPress website. Login issues can be frustrating, but the insights gained from this chapter will empower you to approach login troubleshooting with confidence and efficiency. As you continue your WordPress troubleshooting journey, the knowledge from this chapter will serve as a valuable resource to maintain a secure, user-friendly, and accessible login process, enhancing the overall experience of your website's users and administrators. Happy troubleshooting!

CHAPTER 15: RESOLVING MEDIA UPLOAD PROBLEMS

In this crucial chapter, we explore the common issue of media upload problems in WordPress and provide effective solutions to resolve them. Media files, such as images, videos, and documents, are vital components of a website, and any issues with uploading them can hinder content creation and website functionality. By mastering the art of resolving media upload problems, you'll be empowered to ensure seamless media management and enhance your website's visual appeal.

Identifying Media Upload Problems
Before exploring solutions, it's essential to identify the nature of media upload problems in WordPress. Media upload problems can range from file format issues to server-related limitations.

Solution:
1. *Review Error Messages*: Pay close attention to any error messages displayed during the media upload process. These messages often provide insights into the root cause of the problem.
2. *Check File Formats*: Ensure that you are attempting to upload media files in supported formats. WordPress supports various file types, but certain formats might be restricted based on your website's settings.
3. *Verify File Size Limits*: Confirm the maximum file size allowed for media uploads on your server. If the file size exceeds this limit, it may prevent successful uploads.

Troubleshooting File Format and Size Issues

File format and size issues are common culprits for media upload problems in WordPress.

Solution:

1. **Convert File Formats**: If you encounter issues with specific file formats, convert the media files to supported formats before attempting to upload them.
2. **Compress Large Files**: Use compression tools or plugins to reduce the file size of large media files while maintaining acceptable quality.
3. **Adjust Server Upload Limits**: Increase the maximum upload file size in your server settings to accommodate larger media files.

Resolving File Permissions Problems

Incorrect file permissions can prevent media uploads and cause other issues with media management.

Solution:

1. **Check File and Folder Permissions**: Ensure that the "wp-content/uploads" folder and its subfolders have the correct permissions (usually 755 or 775) to allow media uploads.
2. **Adjust .htaccess File**: Review your website's ".htaccess" file for any misconfigurations that might be affecting file permissions. Consider temporarily disabling it to check if it's causing the issue.
3. **Verify Ownership**: Check the ownership of files and folders on your server to ensure they are associated with the correct user or group.

Handling Server Memory Limitations

Server memory limitations can lead to media upload problems, especially with large files.

Solution:

1. *Increase PHP Memory Limit*: Adjust the PHP memory limit in the "wp-config.php" file to allow more memory for media uploads. Increase the value gradually until the issue is resolved.
2. *Use Chunked Uploads*: Implement chunked uploads using plugins or server configurations. Chunked uploads break large files into smaller pieces, making it easier to handle them with limited memory.
3. *Contact Hosting Provider*: If memory limitations persist, contact your hosting provider to inquire about server memory upgrades or alternative solutions.

Resolving HTTP Error During Uploads

The "HTTP Error" message during media uploads is a common issue that can be challenging to diagnose.

Solution:

1. *Clear Browser Cache*: Instruct users to clear their browser cache and cookies before attempting to upload media files. A cached browser can sometimes cause upload issues.
2. *Disable Security Plugins*: Temporarily disable security plugins that might be interfering with the media upload process. Some security plugins may misidentify legitimate media files as potential threats.
3. *Adjust ModSecurity Rules*: If your server uses ModSecurity, adjust its rules to allow media uploads and prevent false positives.

Addressing Plugin and Theme Conflicts

Conflicts with plugins or themes can affect media uploads in WordPress.

Solution:

1. *Disable Plugins*: Temporarily deactivate all plugins and attempt to upload media. If successful, reactivate plugins one by one to identify the conflicting one.

2. *Switch to a Default Theme*: Temporarily switch to a default WordPress theme to check if the issue is theme-related.
3. *Update Plugins and Themes*: Ensure that all plugins and themes are up to date with their latest versions, as updates often include bug fixes that may resolve upload issues.

Troubleshooting Browser and Network Issues
Browser and network problems can also impact media uploads.

Solution:
1. *Use a Different Browser*: If users encounter upload problems, instruct them to try a different browser to rule out browser-specific issues.
2. *Check Network Connectivity*: Verify that users have a stable internet connection to prevent interruptions during the media upload process.
3. *Disable VPN or Proxy*: If users are using a VPN or proxy, advise them to disable it temporarily as it might affect the upload process.

Conclusion:
In conclusion, this chapter equips you with the expertise to resolve media upload problems effectively. By identifying upload issues, troubleshooting file format and size problems, resolving file permissions issues, handling server memory limitations, addressing HTTP errors during uploads, handling plugin and theme conflicts, and troubleshooting browser and network issues, you'll be well-prepared to ensure smooth media management and enhance the visual content of your WordPress website. Media uploads are crucial for engaging user experiences, and the insights gained from this chapter will empower you to approach media upload troubleshooting with confidence and efficiency. As you continue your WordPress troubleshooting journey, the knowledge from this chapter will serve as a valuable resource to maintain a seamless media

management process, enriching your website with captivating visuals and enhancing overall user satisfaction. Happy uploading!

CHAPTER 16: TROUBLESHOOTING CSS AND STYLING ISSUES

In this essential chapter, we delve into the common CSS and styling issues that can occur in WordPress and explore effective solutions to troubleshoot and resolve them. CSS (Cascading Style Sheets) is fundamental for styling your website, and any problems with CSS can lead to visual inconsistencies and layout errors. By mastering the art of troubleshooting CSS and styling issues, you'll be empowered to maintain a visually appealing and consistent appearance for your WordPress website.

Identifying CSS and Styling Issues
Before exploring solutions, it's crucial to identify the nature of CSS and styling issues in WordPress. Styling problems can include misaligned elements, incorrect colors, missing styles, and more.

Solution:
1. *Review Website Appearance*: Carefully review your website's appearance and compare it to the expected design. Note any discrepancies or visual irregularities.
2. *Use Browser Developer Tools*: Utilize browser developer tools to inspect HTML elements and CSS styles. This helps identify specific CSS rules affecting elements and potential errors.
3. *Check Browser Compatibility*: Verify that your website looks consistent across different web browsers. Some

styling issues may be browser-specific and require targeted fixes.

Troubleshooting Misaligned Elements

Misaligned elements can disrupt your website's layout and diminish its visual appeal.

Solution:

1. *Use CSS Layout Properties*: Utilize CSS layout properties like "margin," "padding," and "position" to align elements correctly on the page.
2. *Check Responsive Design*: Ensure that your website's layout is responsive and adapts to different screen sizes. Test on various devices to verify alignment.
3. *Use Flexbox or Grid Layouts*: Implement Flexbox or CSS Grid to create flexible and responsive layouts, making it easier to align elements consistently.

Fixing Incorrect Colors and Fonts

Incorrect colors or fonts can deviate from your website's intended style and branding.

Solution:

1. *Verify CSS Color Codes*: Double-check CSS color codes used for various elements to ensure they match your desired color scheme.
2. *Check Font Imports*: Review CSS font imports to confirm that the correct fonts are being loaded and displayed on your website.
3. *Use Google Fonts*: Utilize Google Fonts or other reputable font resources to ensure consistent font rendering across different devices and browsers.

Addressing Missing Styles

Missing styles can lead to unstyled or poorly formatted content on your website.

Solution:

1. ***Check CSS File Inclusion***: Verify that your CSS files are correctly included in your WordPress theme's header or footer.
2. ***Review CSS Selectors***: Ensure that CSS selectors are targeting the correct HTML elements to apply styles as intended.
3. ***Check Plugin and Theme Compatibility***: Review plugins and themes for potential conflicts that may cause missing styles. Disable plugins or switch themes to identify the source of the issue.

Handling CSS Overriding and Specificity

CSS overriding and specificity conflicts can cause unexpected styling issues.

Solution:

1. ***Use Specificity Rules***: Employ CSS specificity rules to prioritize styles and prevent unintended overrides. Use "IDs," "classes," and "element types" strategically.
2. ***Avoid Inline Styles***: Minimize the use of inline styles, as they can create specificity conflicts and make CSS management more challenging.
3. ***Review CSS Order***: Arrange CSS rules in a logical order to control how styles are applied. Later rules can override earlier ones, so organize your styles accordingly.

Troubleshooting Browser-Specific Issues

Some CSS and styling issues may be specific to certain web browsers.

Solution:

1. ***Use Browser Prefixes***: Apply browser prefixes ("-webkit-," "-moz-," etc.) to CSS properties for compatibility with specific browsers.
2. ***Test in Multiple Browsers***: Regularly test your website in various web browsers to identify and address browser-

specific styling issues.

3. **Use Browser-Specific CSS Hacks**: As a last resort, consider using targeted CSS hacks to address specific browser issues. Use these cautiously, as they may cause maintenance challenges.

Handling CSS Performance Optimization

Large or unoptimized CSS files can impact your website's loading speed.

Solution:

1. **Minify CSS**: Use CSS minification tools or plugins to remove unnecessary spaces and comments, reducing the size of CSS files.
2. **Leverage CSS Sprites**: Combine small images into CSS sprites to reduce the number of HTTP requests and improve loading times.
3. **Use Critical CSS**: Implement critical CSS techniques to load essential styles first, improving the initial rendering speed of your website.

Conclusion:

In conclusion, this chapter equips you with the expertise to troubleshoot CSS and styling issues effectively. By identifying CSS and styling problems, troubleshooting misaligned elements, fixing incorrect colors and fonts, addressing missing styles, handling CSS overriding and specificity, troubleshooting browser-specific issues, and optimizing CSS performance, you'll be well-prepared to maintain a visually appealing and consistent appearance for your WordPress website. CSS is a powerful tool for website aesthetics, and the insights gained from this chapter will empower you to approach CSS troubleshooting with confidence and efficiency. As you continue your WordPress troubleshooting journey, the knowledge from this chapter will serve as a valuable resource to keep your website visually stunning, user-friendly, and reflective of your brand's identity. Happy styling!

CHAPTER 17: FIXING JAVASCRIPT ERRORS AND CONFLICTS

In this critical chapter, we explore the common JavaScript errors and conflicts that can arise in WordPress and provide effective solutions to troubleshoot and resolve them. JavaScript is a fundamental scripting language for website interactivity and functionality, and any issues with JavaScript can lead to broken features and unpredictable behavior. By mastering the art of fixing JavaScript errors and conflicts, you'll be empowered to ensure a smooth and seamless user experience on your WordPress website.

Identifying JavaScript Errors
Before exploring solutions, it's crucial to identify the nature of JavaScript errors in WordPress. JavaScript errors can occur due to syntax mistakes, missing files, or incompatible code.

Solution:
1. *Use Browser Developer Tools*: Utilize browser developer tools to inspect JavaScript console messages. These tools provide valuable information about JavaScript errors and their sources.
2. *Check Theme and Plugin Code*: Review the code of your active theme and plugins for any JavaScript syntax errors or conflicts.
3. *Monitor User Feedback*: Pay attention to user feedback regarding broken features or unexpected behavior, as

it might indicate JavaScript errors.

Troubleshooting Syntax Errors

JavaScript syntax errors can disrupt the execution of scripts on your website.

Solution:

1. *Use Code Linters*: Utilize code linters or syntax checkers to automatically identify and highlight syntax errors in your JavaScript code.
2. *Review Code Changes*: If the error occurred after making code changes, carefully review the modified code for any typos or syntax mistakes.
3. *Check Brackets and Parentheses*: Verify that all brackets and parentheses in your JavaScript code are correctly matched and closed.

Handling Missing JavaScript Files

Missing JavaScript files can lead to broken functionality on your website.

Solution:

1. *Verify File Paths*: Double-check the file paths for your JavaScript files to ensure they are correctly specified in the HTML or PHP files.
2. *Check File Uploads*: If you recently updated your theme or plugins, ensure that all associated JavaScript files were uploaded correctly to your server.
3. *Reinstall Theme or Plugin*: If missing JavaScript files are caused by incomplete updates, consider reinstalling the theme or plugin to ensure all necessary files are present.

Resolving JavaScript Conflicts

Conflicts between multiple JavaScript libraries or scripts can cause unexpected behavior.

Solution:

1. *Check Console for Clashes*: Inspect the browser console for any error messages related to conflicting JavaScript libraries or scripts.
2. *Disable Plugins*: Temporarily deactivate plugins to identify if a specific plugin is causing JavaScript conflicts.
3. *Use jQuery No-Conflict Mode*: If using multiple JavaScript libraries, employ jQuery no-conflict mode to prevent conflicts with other JavaScript libraries using the "$" symbol.

Handling Asynchronous Loading Issues
Asynchronous loading of JavaScript can cause timing-related conflicts.

Solution:
1. *Use "defer" and "async"*: When including external JavaScript files, utilize the "defer" or "async" attributes to control the loading order and prevent timing conflicts.
2. *Load Dependencies First*: Ensure that JavaScript files depending on other scripts or libraries are loaded after their dependencies.
3. *Minimize Inline JavaScript*: Reduce the use of inline JavaScript and move scripts to external files with proper loading attributes.

Troubleshooting Browser Compatibility
Some JavaScript errors and conflicts may be browser-specific.

Solution:
1. *Use Browser Developer Tools*: Utilize browser developer tools to identify JavaScript errors occurring only in specific browsers.
2. *Check Compatibility Tables*: Refer to browser compatibility tables and documentation to identify unsupported JavaScript features.

3. ***Implement Polyfills***: Use polyfills to provide fallback solutions for unsupported JavaScript features in specific browsers.

Updating JavaScript Libraries

Outdated JavaScript libraries can lead to security vulnerabilities and compatibility issues.

Solution:

1. ***Regularly Update Libraries***: Keep JavaScript libraries and frameworks up to date with their latest versions to ensure optimal performance and security.
2. ***Check Library Deprecation***: Verify if any used JavaScript libraries are deprecated and migrate to supported alternatives.
3. ***Test Updates Locally***: Before updating JavaScript libraries on your live website, test the updates on a local development environment to identify potential issues.

Conclusion:

In conclusion, this chapter equips you with the expertise to fix JavaScript errors and conflicts effectively. By identifying JavaScript errors, troubleshooting syntax errors, handling missing JavaScript files, resolving JavaScript conflicts, addressing asynchronous loading issues, troubleshooting browser compatibility, and updating JavaScript libraries, you'll be well-prepared to ensure a smooth and seamless user experience on your WordPress website. JavaScript is a powerful tool for website interactivity, and the insights gained from this chapter will empower you to approach JavaScript troubleshooting with confidence and efficiency. As you continue your WordPress troubleshooting journey, the knowledge from this chapter will serve as a valuable resource to maintain functional and interactive website elements, enhancing user engagement and overall website performance. Happy scripting!

CHAPTER 18: SOLVING WORDPRESS EMAIL ISSUES

In this essential chapter, we address the common WordPress email issues that users may encounter and explore effective solutions to troubleshoot and resolve them. Email functionality in WordPress is vital for user communication, password reset notifications, and other essential notifications. Any problems with WordPress email can result in users not receiving crucial messages, impacting user engagement and website functionality. By mastering the art of solving WordPress email issues, you'll be empowered to ensure reliable and efficient email communication on your WordPress website.

Identifying WordPress Email Issues
Before exploring solutions, it's crucial to identify the nature of WordPress email issues. Email problems can range from emails not being delivered to users not receiving notifications.

Solution:
1. *Check Email Logs*: Utilize email logs or email tracking plugins to review the status and delivery details of sent emails.
2. *Test Email Functionality*: Conduct email tests on various scenarios, such as user registration, password reset, and contact forms, to identify issues.
3. *Monitor User Feedback*: Pay attention to user feedback regarding email-related problems, as it may reveal patterns or specific issues.

Troubleshooting Email Delivery Problems

Email delivery problems can occur due to various factors, including server configurations and spam filtering.

Solution:

1. *Verify Mail Server Settings*: Double-check your WordPress site's mail server settings and ensure they are correctly configured for sending emails.
2. *Use SMTP for Sending Emails*: Implement SMTP (Simple Mail Transfer Protocol) to send emails from your WordPress site. SMTP is more reliable than the default PHP mail function and less likely to be flagged as spam.
3. *Check Spam Folder*: Advise users to check their spam or junk folders if they are not receiving expected emails from your WordPress website.

Handling Email Blacklisting and Spam Issues

WordPress email can be marked as spam if sent excessively or if the server's IP is blacklisted.

Solution:

1. *Monitor Email Frequency*: Avoid sending excessive emails in a short period to prevent being flagged as spam by email providers.
2. *Check Server IP Blacklists*: Regularly check if your server's IP address is blacklisted by email providers. If blacklisted, contact your hosting provider for resolution.
3. *Implement Email Double Opt-In*: Use double opt-in for email subscriptions to ensure users genuinely want to receive emails from your website, reducing the chances of spam complaints.

Resolving Email Template and Content Problems

Issues with email templates and content can result in poorly formatted or incomplete emails.

Solution:
1. *Customize Email Templates*: Customize your WordPress email templates to match your website's branding and ensure professional and consistent communication.
2. *Review Dynamic Content*: Check for dynamic content placeholders in email templates, ensuring they are correctly replaced with relevant information (e.g., user names, links).
3. *Test Email Rendering*: Test email rendering on various email clients and devices to ensure the emails appear as intended.

Fixing Email Bounce Backs

Email bounce backs occur when emails fail to reach the recipient due to invalid or unreachable email addresses.

Solution:
1. *Clean Email Lists*: Regularly clean your email lists to remove invalid or inactive email addresses, reducing bounce back rates.
2. *Implement Bounce Handling*: Utilize bounce handling systems or plugins to automatically remove bouncing email addresses from your lists.
3. *Use Double Opt-In for Subscribers*: Employ double opt-in to ensure the validity of email addresses before adding them to your subscriber list.

Troubleshooting Email Attachments

Issues with email attachments can hinder users from receiving important files or documents.

Solution:
1. *Check Attachment File Types*: Verify that the allowed file types for email attachments are correctly specified to accommodate the desired files.
2. *Increase Attachment Size Limit*: Increase the maximum attachment size limit in your email settings if users

encounter issues with large attachments.

3. *Use File Upload Plugins*: For complex file handling, consider using file upload plugins to manage email attachments more efficiently.

Handling Email Deliverability and DNS Settings
Incorrect DNS settings can affect email deliverability and cause issues with verification.

Solution:

1. *Set Up SPF and DKIM*: Implement SPF (Sender Policy Framework) and DKIM (DomainKeys Identified Mail) to improve email deliverability and authentication.
2. *Verify MX Records*: Ensure that your domain's MX (Mail Exchange) records are correctly configured for smooth email delivery.
3. *Use Email Delivery Services*: Consider using third-party email delivery services for more reliable email delivery and advanced tracking features.

Conclusion:
In conclusion, this chapter equips you with the expertise to solve WordPress email issues effectively. By identifying email delivery problems, troubleshooting email blacklisting and spam issues, handling email template and content problems, resolving email bounce backs, fixing email attachments, and addressing email deliverability and DNS settings, you'll be well-prepared to ensure reliable and efficient email communication on your WordPress website. Email functionality is essential for user engagement, and the insights gained from this chapter will empower you to approach WordPress email troubleshooting with confidence and efficiency. As you continue your WordPress troubleshooting journey, the knowledge from this chapter will serve as a valuable resource to maintain effective email communication, enhance user engagement, and promote a seamless user experience on your WordPress website. Happy emailing!

CHAPTER 19: TROUBLESHOOTING MOBILE RESPONSIVENESS

In this pivotal chapter, we delve into the common issues related to mobile responsiveness in WordPress and provide effective solutions to troubleshoot and resolve them. Mobile responsiveness is critical in today's digital landscape, as an increasing number of users access websites on mobile devices. Any problems with mobile responsiveness can lead to a poor user experience and deter mobile visitors from engaging with your website. By mastering the art of troubleshooting mobile responsiveness, you'll be empowered to ensure a seamless and visually appealing experience for all users, regardless of the device they use to access your WordPress website.

Identifying Mobile Responsiveness Issues
Before exploring solutions, it's crucial to identify the nature of mobile responsiveness issues in WordPress. Mobile responsiveness problems can include elements not scaling correctly, content cutoff, or elements overlapping on smaller screens.

Solution:
1. *Use Responsive Testing Tools*: Utilize responsive testing tools or browser developer tools to preview your website on various screen sizes and identify mobile responsiveness issues.
2. *Test on Different Devices*: Regularly test your website

on different mobile devices to ensure a consistent user experience across various screen sizes and resolutions.

3. *Analyze User Behavior*: Analyze user behavior through website analytics to identify any patterns of high bounce rates or low engagement on mobile devices.

Troubleshooting CSS Media Queries

CSS media queries control how your website adapts to different screen sizes and are fundamental for mobile responsiveness.

Solution:

1. *Review Media Query Rules*: Check your CSS media query rules to ensure they target the correct screen sizes and breakpoints.
2. *Adjust Breakpoints*: Fine-tune your media query breakpoints to ensure a smooth transition between different screen sizes.
3. *Use Mobile-First Approach*: Implement a mobile-first approach in your CSS by styling for smaller screens first and progressively enhancing the design for larger screens.

Handling Image Optimization for Mobile

Unoptimized images can slow down mobile loading times and impact mobile responsiveness.

Solution:

1. *Compress Images*: Use image compression tools or plugins to reduce image file sizes without sacrificing quality.
2. *Use Responsive Images*: Implement responsive image techniques, such as the "srcset" attribute, to serve different image sizes based on the user's device.
3. *Lazy Load Images*: Employ lazy loading for images, allowing them to load as the user scrolls, reducing initial page load times.

Fixing Font and Text Size Issues

Incorrect font sizes and text scaling can lead to readability problems on mobile devices.

Solution:

1. *Use Relative Font Sizes*: Use relative font sizes (e.g., "em" or "rem") instead of fixed pixel sizes to ensure text scales appropriately on different screen sizes.
2. *Test Font Legibility*: Test font legibility on various mobile devices to ensure text remains readable at different font sizes.
3. *Avoid Text Overflows*: Prevent text overflow issues by setting appropriate line heights and avoiding long unbroken lines of text.

Resolving Navigation and Menu Problems

Navigation and menu elements can be challenging to navigate on smaller screens.

Solution:

1. *Implement Responsive Menus*: Use responsive menu techniques, such as collapsible or off-canvas menus, to provide a user-friendly navigation experience on mobile devices.
2. *Optimize Touch Targets*: Ensure that menu items and navigation links have sufficient spacing and size to accommodate touch interactions on mobile screens.
3. *Test Navigation Flow*: Test the entire navigation flow on different mobile devices to verify a seamless user experience.

Troubleshooting Touchscreen Interactions

Certain interactive elements may not work correctly on touchscreen devices.

Solution:

1. *Implement Touch-Friendly Features*: Use touch-friendly features like swipe gestures or tap interactions for sliders, carousels, and other interactive elements.

2. ***Test Touchscreen Compatibility***: Regularly test interactive elements on touchscreen devices to ensure they function as expected.
3. ***Provide Alternative Interactions***: Offer alternative interactions for elements that may not work optimally on touchscreens.

Handling Mobile Page Speed

Page speed is crucial for mobile users, as slow loading times can lead to high bounce rates.

Solution:

1. ***Optimize CSS and JavaScript***: Minify and concatenate CSS and JavaScript files to reduce the number of HTTP requests and improve page loading speed.
2. ***Use Caching and Content Delivery Networks (CDNs)***: Implement caching plugins and use CDNs to serve static assets from servers closer to the user, enhancing page speed.
3. ***Test Mobile Page Speed***: Regularly test your website's mobile page speed using tools like Google PageSpeed Insights and make necessary optimizations.

Conclusion:

In conclusion, this chapter equips you with the expertise to troubleshoot mobile responsiveness effectively. By identifying mobile responsiveness issues, troubleshooting CSS media queries, handling image optimization, fixing font and text size issues, resolving navigation and menu problems, addressing touchscreen interactions, and handling mobile page speed, you'll be well-prepared to ensure a seamless and visually engaging experience for mobile users on your WordPress website. Mobile responsiveness is critical for user engagement and website success, and the insights gained from this chapter will empower you to approach mobile responsiveness troubleshooting with confidence and efficiency. As you continue your WordPress troubleshooting journey, the knowledge from this chapter will serve as a valuable resource to enhance mobile user experiences, increase user engagement, and optimize the overall performance of your WordPress website on various mobile devices. Happy troubleshooting!

CHAPTER 20: RECOVERING LOST OR DELETED CONTENT

In this critical chapter, we address the distressing scenario of lost or deleted content in WordPress and provide effective solutions to recover and restore it. Content is the heart of any WordPress website, and accidental deletions or data loss can be devastating for website owners and administrators. By mastering the art of recovering lost or deleted content, you'll be empowered to mitigate the impact of such incidents and maintain the integrity of your WordPress website.

Identifying Lost or Deleted Content
Before exploring solutions, it's crucial to identify the extent of lost or deleted content in WordPress. Content loss can range from single posts or pages to entire sections or databases.

Solution:
1. ***Check Recently Deleted Items***: Check your website's trash or recently deleted items to identify any content that may have been unintentionally removed.
2. ***Review Revision History***: Utilize WordPress's built-in revision history feature to track changes made to posts and pages and identify when content might have been lost.
3. ***Analyze Server Backups***: Review your server backups to identify the last known state of the website before the content loss occurred.

Recovering from the Trash or Recycle Bin

Content that has been deleted may still be recoverable from the WordPress trash or recycle bin.

Solution:

1. **Restore from Trash**: If content is found in the trash, simply restore it to its original location using the "Restore" option.
2. **Check Trash Expiration**: Confirm the trash expiration settings in WordPress to ensure deleted items are retained for a sufficient period before permanent deletion.
3. **Use Bulk Restore**: In case of multiple deleted items, use bulk restore functionality to recover content more efficiently.

Retrieving from Revisions or Autosave

Lost or unsaved changes can be retrieved using WordPress's revision history or autosave feature.

Solution:

1. **Use Revision History**: Access the revision history of a post or page to restore previous versions that contain the content you want to recover.
2. **Check Autosave Versions**: If you encountered an unexpected crash or loss of unsaved changes, check the autosave versions to retrieve the most recent content.
3. **Manually Copy Content**: If you can't retrieve content from revisions or autosaves, manually copy content from backups or any other available sources.

Restoring from Server Backups

Server backups are valuable lifelines in recovering lost or deleted content.

Solution:

1. **Locate Backup Copies**: Access your server backups and locate the most recent backup that contains the content you need to restore.

2. **Use Backup Restoration Tools**: Depending on your hosting environment, utilize backup restoration tools or plugins to restore specific content or entire databases.

3. **Verify Backup Integrity**: Ensure the integrity of your backups by performing test restorations on a local server before proceeding with a live website restoration.

Seeking Professional Assistance

In complex scenarios or if backups are unavailable, seeking professional help may be necessary.

Solution:

1. **Contact Hosting Support**: Reach out to your hosting provider's support team to inquire about available backup options or professional restoration services.

2. **Hire WordPress Experts**: Consider hiring WordPress experts or developers who specialize in data recovery and website restoration.

3. **Use WordPress Data Recovery Services**: Explore WordPress data recovery services that specialize in retrieving lost or deleted content from WordPress databases.

Implementing Preventive Measures

To avoid future content loss incidents, implement preventive measures for data protection.

Solution:

1. **Regular Backups**: Schedule regular backups of your WordPress website, including both the database and the entire file system.

2. **Use Backup Plugins**: Utilize reputable backup plugins that automate the backup process and offer easy restoration options.

3. **Train Website Administrators**: Educate website

administrators about best practices for content management and the use of revision history to prevent accidental deletions.

Conclusion:

In conclusion, this chapter equips you with the expertise to recover lost or deleted content effectively. By identifying lost or deleted content, recovering from the trash or recycle bin, retrieving from revisions or autosave, restoring from server backups, seeking professional assistance when needed, and implementing preventive measures, you'll be well-prepared to handle content loss incidents with confidence and efficiency. Content is the lifeblood of a WordPress website, and the insights gained from this chapter will empower you to safeguard and restore valuable content, ensuring the continuity and success of your WordPress website. As you continue your WordPress troubleshooting journey, the knowledge from this chapter will serve as a valuable resource to protect against data loss and maintain the integrity of your website's content for a seamless user experience. Happy recovering!

CHAPTER 21: RESOLVING WORDPRESS MULTISITE PROBLEMS

In this crucial chapter, we tackle the common issues related to WordPress Multisite and provide effective solutions to troubleshoot and resolve them. WordPress Multisite is a powerful feature that allows users to manage multiple websites from a single WordPress installation. However, managing a multisite network comes with its own set of challenges, including configuration errors, access restrictions, and performance issues. By mastering the art of resolving WordPress Multisite problems, you'll be empowered to maintain a smooth and efficient multisite network, ensuring optimal performance and user experience across all websites within the network.

Identifying WordPress Multisite Problems
Before exploring solutions, it's crucial to identify the nature of WordPress Multisite problems. Multisite issues can range from configuration errors to compatibility conflicts.

Solution:
1. *Check Multisite Network Dashboard*: Review the Multisite network dashboard for any error messages or warnings that might indicate issues.
2. *Monitor User Feedback*: Pay attention to user feedback from different websites within the Multisite network to identify common problems experienced by users.

3. *Review Server Logs*: Examine server logs for any error messages or notices related to the Multisite network.

Troubleshooting Network Setup and Configuration
Errors during the setup or configuration of the Multisite network can impact its functionality.

Solution:

1. *Review wp-config.php*: Check the "wp-config.php" file for any misconfigurations or missing constants related to the Multisite setup.
2. *Verify .htaccess Rules*: Ensure that the .htaccess file has the correct rules for the Multisite network, as incorrect rules can cause various issues.
3. *Rebuild Permalinks*: If you encounter permalink-related issues, rebuild the permalinks by navigating to "Settings > Permalinks" in the network dashboard.

Handling Domain Mapping and SSL Issues
Domain mapping and SSL configuration can be challenging in a WordPress Multisite network.

Solution:

1. *Check Domain Mapping Settings*: Review domain mapping settings and verify that domain mappings are correctly associated with respective websites.
2. *Use Valid SSL Certificates*: Ensure that SSL certificates are correctly installed and valid for mapped domains to secure connections.
3. *Update URLs in Database*: If domain mapping issues persist, update the URLs in the database for the affected websites using appropriate migration plugins or SQL queries.

Resolving Access and Permissions Problems
Issues with user access and permissions can restrict website administrators from managing their sites.

Solution:

1. *Verify User Roles*: Confirm that user roles are correctly assigned within the Multisite network, granting appropriate access and capabilities.
2. *Check Site Privacy Settings*: If specific websites are inaccessible to users, check the site privacy settings in the network dashboard.
3. *Review User Registration Settings*: Ensure that user registration settings are configured to allow or restrict new user registrations as desired.

Troubleshooting Plugin and Theme Compatibility
Compatibility issues with plugins and themes can cause errors in the Multisite network.

Solution:

1. *Use Multisite Compatible Plugins*: Choose plugins explicitly designed to work with WordPress Multisite, reducing the risk of conflicts.
2. *Test Themes for Compatibility*: Verify that themes used across the network are compatible with WordPress Multisite and do not cause layout or functionality issues.
3. *Disable Problematic Plugins or Themes*: Temporarily disable plugins or themes that cause conflicts, and seek alternative solutions or replacements.

Handling Performance and Scalability Concerns
As the Multisite network grows, performance and scalability become significant concerns.

Solution:

1. *Use Caching and CDN*: Implement caching and content delivery networks (CDNs) to enhance the performance of the Multisite network.
2. *Optimize Database*: Regularly optimize the database of the Multisite network to improve query performance.

3. *Consider Server Upgrades*: Evaluate the need for server upgrades or specialized hosting solutions to handle increased traffic and data.

Troubleshooting Multisite Backup and Restoration
Backup and restoration processes are essential for maintaining data integrity in a Multisite network.

Solution:
1. *Use Multisite Backup Plugins*: Employ backup plugins designed specifically for WordPress Multisite networks to ensure comprehensive data protection.
2. *Test Backup Restorations*: Periodically test backup restoration on a local server to confirm that the process works flawlessly when needed.
3. *Maintain Off-Site Backups*: Store backup files in off-site locations to safeguard data in the event of server failures or disasters.

Conclusion:
In conclusion, this chapter equips you with the expertise to resolve WordPress Multisite problems effectively. By identifying Multisite issues, troubleshooting network setup and configuration, handling domain mapping and SSL issues, resolving access and permissions problems, addressing plugin and theme compatibility, handling performance and scalability concerns, and troubleshooting Multisite backup and restoration, you'll be well-prepared to manage a seamless and efficient Multisite network. WordPress Multisite is a powerful tool for managing multiple websites, and the insights gained from this chapter will empower you to tackle Multisite-related challenges with confidence and efficiency. As you continue your WordPress troubleshooting journey, the knowledge from this chapter will serve as a valuable resource to maintain a stable and high-performing Multisite network, enhancing website management and user experience across all sites within the network. Happy Multisite troubleshooting!

CHAPTER 22: FIXING BROKEN REDIRECTS

In this essential chapter, we delve into the issue of broken redirects in WordPress and provide effective solutions to troubleshoot and fix them. Redirects are crucial for maintaining the SEO value of your website and ensuring a seamless user experience. However, broken redirects can lead to frustrating 404 errors and negatively impact your website's search engine rankings. By mastering the art of fixing broken redirects, you'll be empowered to maintain a well-structured and user-friendly website, enhancing user satisfaction and search engine visibility.

Identifying Broken Redirects
Before exploring solutions, it's crucial to identify broken redirects in WordPress. Broken redirects can occur due to incorrect configurations or changes in permalink structures.

Solution:
1. *Use Redirect Tracking Tools*: Utilize redirect tracking tools or plugins to identify broken redirects and receive notifications of 404 errors.
2. *Monitor Webmaster Tools*: Check your website's webmaster tools (e.g., Google Search Console) for crawl error reports that highlight broken redirects.
3. *Review Website Analytics*: Analyze website analytics for patterns of incoming traffic from broken redirect URLs.

Troubleshooting Redirect Configuration Errors
Incorrect configurations in redirect settings can result in broken redirects.

Solution:
1. *Check Redirection Plugin Settings*: If you're using a redirection plugin, review its settings to ensure that redirects are correctly configured.
2. *Verify .htaccess Rules*: For manual redirects, verify that the .htaccess file contains the correct redirection rules and that they are not conflicting.
3. *Test Redirects Manually*: Manually test each redirect to confirm they lead to the intended destinations and do not result in 404 errors.

Handling Changes in Permalink Structure
Changes in permalink structure can lead to broken redirects if not managed correctly.

Solution:
1. *Implement Proper Permalink Changes*: If you need to change the permalink structure, use the appropriate methods (e.g., setting up 301 redirects) to preserve SEO value and prevent broken links.
2. *Update Internal Links*: After changing the permalink structure, update internal links within your content to reflect the new URLs.
3. *Use Canonical Tags*: Implement canonical tags to inform search engines about the preferred URL version and avoid duplicate content issues.

Addressing Expired Redirects
Redirects to expired or obsolete URLs can result in broken redirects.

Solution:
1. *Regularly Review Redirects*: Periodically review your

website's redirects and update or remove any redirects leading to expired URLs.

2. *Set Expiration Dates*: If using a redirection plugin, set expiration dates for temporary redirects to automatically remove them when they are no longer needed.

3. *Use 410 Status Code*: For permanently expired URLs, use the 410 Gone status code to inform search engines that the page no longer exists.

Fixing Incorrect Domain Redirects
Issues with domain redirection can cause broken redirects.

Solution:

1. *Verify Domain Mapping Settings*: Review domain mapping settings to ensure that mapped domains are correctly associated with the intended websites.

2. *Check DNS Settings*: Verify DNS settings for domain mapping and ensure that they point to the correct server.

3. *Use Redirect Chains*: For complex domain redirects, use redirect chains to route traffic properly and avoid broken redirects.

Implementing a Robust Redirect Maintenance Plan
To prevent future broken redirects, implement a comprehensive redirect maintenance plan.

Solution:

1. *Regularly Monitor Redirects*: Continuously monitor your website's redirects and promptly address any new instances of broken redirects.

2. *Test After Website Changes*: After making significant changes to your website's structure or content, test redirects to ensure they remain functional.

3. *Set Up Alerts*: Configure alerts or notifications to receive immediate updates when broken redirects are

detected.

Conclusion:

In conclusion, this chapter equips you with the expertise to fix broken redirects effectively. By identifying broken redirects, troubleshooting redirect configuration errors, handling changes in permalink structure, addressing expired redirects, fixing incorrect domain redirects, and implementing a robust redirect maintenance plan, you'll be well-prepared to maintain a well-structured and user-friendly website. Redirects are vital for preserving SEO value and providing a seamless user experience, and the insights gained from this chapter will empower you to approach redirect troubleshooting with confidence and efficiency. As you continue your WordPress troubleshooting journey, the knowledge from this chapter will serve as a valuable resource to ensure that your website's redirects are functional, enhancing user satisfaction and search engine rankings. Happy redirect fixing!

CHAPTER 23: TROUBLESHOOTING WOOCOMMERCE INTEGRATION

In this crucial chapter, we delve into the intricacies of troubleshooting WooCommerce integration in WordPress and provide effective solutions to address common issues. WooCommerce is a popular e-commerce plugin that adds powerful online store capabilities to your WordPress website. However, integrating WooCommerce can introduce various challenges, such as payment gateway errors, inventory management issues, and product display problems. By mastering the art of troubleshooting WooCommerce integration, you'll be empowered to create a seamless and successful e-commerce experience for your customers, driving sales and business growth.

Identifying WooCommerce Integration Issues
Before exploring solutions, it's crucial to identify the nature of WooCommerce integration issues. Integration problems can range from payment processing errors to misconfigured product settings.

Solution:
1. ***Review Error Logs***: Check WooCommerce error logs or server logs for any error messages or notices related to

the integration.
2. *Monitor Customer Feedback*: Pay attention to customer feedback and support requests to identify recurring issues with the e-commerce functionality.
3. *Verify Plugin Compatibility*: Ensure that all installed plugins are compatible with WooCommerce to prevent conflicts and integration problems.

Troubleshooting Payment Gateway Errors
Payment gateway errors can hinder smooth transactions on your WooCommerce store.

Solution:
1. *Check Payment Gateway Settings*: Review the settings of your selected payment gateway to ensure that the credentials and configurations are accurate.
2. *Test Transactions*: Conduct test transactions with different payment methods to identify and resolve any issues with payment processing.
3. *Use Trusted Payment Gateways*: Choose well-established and reputable payment gateways that are known for reliability and security.

Handling Inventory and Product Management Problems
Inventory management and product display issues can disrupt the e-commerce experience.

Solution:
1. *Review Product Settings*: Check product settings to ensure that inventory tracking, stock status, and product visibility are correctly configured.
2. *Update Product Information*: Regularly update product details, prices, and availability to avoid any discrepancies between your website and physical inventory.
3. **Use Inventory Management Plugins**: Employ inventory management plugins to automate

stock tracking and synchronization with your WooCommerce store.

Fixing Shipping and Tax Calculation Errors

Shipping and tax calculation errors can lead to inaccurate pricing for customers.

Solution:

1. *Verify Shipping Settings*: Review shipping methods and rates in WooCommerce settings to ensure they align with your business requirements.
2. *Test Shipping Rates*: Conduct test orders with different shipping addresses to verify that shipping rates are calculated accurately.
3. *Set Up Tax Rules Correctly*: Configure tax rules and rates according to your business location and relevant tax laws.

Troubleshooting Theme and Design Compatibility

Compatibility issues between WooCommerce and your theme can impact the layout and functionality of your store.

Solution:

1. *Use WooCommerce-Compatible Themes*: Select themes that explicitly state WooCommerce compatibility to ensure smooth integration.
2. *Review Styling Conflicts*: Check for CSS conflicts between your theme and WooCommerce elements, and make necessary adjustments to maintain a consistent design.
3. *Test Responsive Design*: Test your WooCommerce store on various devices to ensure responsive design and optimal user experience.

Handling Slow Loading and Performance Issues

Slow loading times and performance problems can deter customers from completing their purchases.

Solution:

1. *Use Caching and CDNs*: Implement caching plugins and content delivery networks (CDNs) to improve page loading times.
2. *Optimize Product Images*: Compress and optimize product images to reduce their file sizes and improve overall site performance.
3. *Review Hosting Resources*: Ensure that your hosting resources are adequate to handle the e-commerce traffic and resource-intensive tasks.

Troubleshooting Order Processing and Customer Notifications
Issues with order processing and customer notifications can result in unsatisfied customers.

Solution:

1. *Test Order Placement*: Conduct test orders to verify that the order processing and confirmation emails are working correctly.
2. *Check Email Deliverability*: Ensure that WooCommerce emails are delivered to customers' inboxes and not marked as spam.
3. *Customize Email Templates*: Personalize email templates to match your brand and enhance the customer experience.

Conclusion:
In conclusion, this chapter equips you with the expertise to troubleshoot WooCommerce integration effectively. By identifying WooCommerce integration issues, troubleshooting payment gateway errors, handling inventory and product management problems, fixing shipping and tax calculation errors, addressing theme and design compatibility, handling slow loading and performance issues, and troubleshooting order processing and customer notifications, you'll be well-prepared to create a seamless and successful e-commerce

experience for your customers. WooCommerce is a powerful e-commerce plugin, and the insights gained from this chapter will empower you to approach WooCommerce integration troubleshooting with confidence and efficiency. As you continue your WordPress troubleshooting journey, the knowledge from this chapter will serve as a valuable resource to optimize your WooCommerce store, boost sales, and enhance customer satisfaction. Happy WooCommerce troubleshooting!

CHAPTER 24: ADDRESSING WORDPRESS SEO ISSUES

In this pivotal chapter, we explore the critical task of addressing WordPress SEO issues and provide effective solutions to optimize your website for search engines. Search engine optimization (SEO) is fundamental for increasing organic traffic and improving your website's visibility on search engine results pages. However, various factors can hinder your SEO efforts, including poor content optimization, technical issues, and crawlability problems. By mastering the art of addressing WordPress SEO issues, you'll be empowered to enhance your website's search engine rankings, attract more organic traffic, and boost your online presence.

Identifying WordPress SEO Issues

Before exploring solutions, it's crucial to identify the nature of SEO issues on your WordPress website. SEO problems can range from low-ranking keywords to poor website structure.

Solution:

1. *Conduct SEO Audits*: Use SEO audit tools or plugins to perform comprehensive assessments of your website's SEO health.
2. *Analyze Search Analytics*: Review search analytics and website traffic data to identify trends and areas of improvement.
3. *Use Webmaster Tools*: Utilize webmaster tools, such as Google Search Console, to identify crawl errors and other SEO-related issues.

Troubleshooting Keyword Optimization

Inadequate keyword optimization can result in poor search engine rankings and lower organic traffic.

Solution:

1. *Keyword Research*: Conduct thorough keyword research to identify relevant and high-traffic keywords for your content.
2. *Use Target Keywords Strategically*: Incorporate target keywords naturally into your content, meta tags, and headings.
3. *Avoid Keyword Stuffing*: Avoid overusing keywords, as keyword stuffing can lead to search engine penalties.

Handling Content Quality and Relevance

Low-quality or irrelevant content can negatively impact your website's SEO performance.

Solution:

1. *Create High-Quality Content*: Focus on producing valuable, informative, and engaging content that meets the needs of your target audience.
2. *Optimize Content Structure*: Use descriptive headings, bullet points, and relevant internal links to enhance content structure and user experience.
3. *Update Outdated Content*: Regularly review and update outdated content to ensure its accuracy and relevance.

Fixing Duplicate Content Issues

Duplicate content can confuse search engines and dilute the authority of your website.

Solution:

1. *Use Canonical Tags*: Implement canonical tags to indicate the preferred version of duplicate content to search engines.
2. *Consolidate Similar Pages*: Merge similar pages or

articles to avoid duplicate content issues.

3. *Set Indexing Preferences*: Configure indexing preferences in robots.txt or meta tags to prevent search engines from indexing duplicate content.

Addressing Website Speed and Performance

Slow loading times can negatively impact user experience and search engine rankings.

Solution:

1. *Use Caching Plugins*: Install caching plugins to improve website loading times by serving cached content to visitors.
2. *Optimize Images*: Compress and optimize images to reduce their file sizes without compromising visual quality.
3. *Minify CSS and JavaScript*: Minify CSS and JavaScript files to reduce their size and improve website performance.

Troubleshooting Technical SEO Issues

Technical SEO issues can hinder search engine crawlers from accessing and indexing your website properly.

Solution:

1. *Check Robots.txt*: Verify that your robots.txt file does not block search engine crawlers from accessing important pages.
2. *Use XML Sitemaps*: Create and submit XML sitemaps to search engines to help them discover and index your website's content.
3. *Resolve 404 Errors*: Identify and fix broken links or missing pages that result in 404 errors.

Handling Mobile-Friendly Optimization

Mobile-friendly websites receive preferential treatment in search engine rankings.

Solution:

1. ***Use Responsive Design***: Implement a responsive design that automatically adapts to different screen sizes and devices.
2. ***Test Mobile Usability***: Regularly test your website's mobile usability using Google's Mobile-Friendly Test tool.
3. ***Optimize Touch Elements***: Ensure that buttons and links are easily tappable on mobile devices.

Conclusion:

In conclusion, this chapter equips you with the expertise to address WordPress SEO issues effectively. By identifying SEO issues, troubleshooting keyword optimization, handling content quality and relevance, fixing duplicate content issues, addressing website speed and performance, troubleshooting technical SEO issues, and handling mobile-friendly optimization, you'll be well-prepared to optimize your website for search engines and attract more organic traffic. SEO is crucial for the success of your WordPress website, and the insights gained from this chapter will empower you to approach SEO troubleshooting with confidence and efficiency. As you continue your WordPress troubleshooting journey, the knowledge from this chapter will serve as a valuable resource to improve your website's search engine rankings, visibility, and overall online presence. Happy SEO troubleshooting!

CHAPTER 25: SOLVING BROWSER COMPATIBILITY PROBLEMS

In this crucial chapter, we address the challenges of browser compatibility in WordPress and provide effective solutions to ensure your website displays correctly across different web browsers. Browser compatibility is essential for delivering a consistent user experience to visitors using various browsers, devices, and operating systems. However, variations in browser rendering engines and support for web standards can lead to layout issues and functionality problems. By mastering the art of solving browser compatibility problems, you'll be empowered to create a seamless and user-friendly website accessible to a broader audience.

Identifying Browser Compatibility Issues
Before exploring solutions, it's crucial to identify the nature of browser compatibility issues on your WordPress website. Compatibility problems can manifest as layout discrepancies, broken functionalities, or design inconsistencies.

Solution:
1. *Use Browser Testing Tools*: Utilize browser testing tools or online services to view your website across multiple browsers and versions.
2. *Monitor User Feedback*: Pay attention to user feedback and support requests related to browser-specific issues.

3. *Conduct Cross-Browser Testing*: Regularly conduct cross-browser testing to identify and resolve compatibility problems proactively.

Ensuring CSS and HTML Standards Compliance

CSS and HTML code that doesn't adhere to web standards can lead to browser rendering inconsistencies.

Solution:

1. *Use Valid CSS and HTML*: Ensure that your CSS and HTML code is valid and compliant with W3C web standards.
2. *Check Vendor Prefixes*: Verify that any vendor-specific CSS prefixes are correctly used to support different browser versions.
3. *Test Custom CSS*: If you have custom CSS, test it across browsers to identify any conflicts or rendering issues.

Handling JavaScript Compatibility

Browser variations in JavaScript support can cause functionality problems on your website.

Solution:

1. *Use Cross-Browser Compatible JavaScript Libraries*: Prefer widely used JavaScript libraries that have built-in cross-browser compatibility.
2. *Implement Feature Detection*: Use feature detection techniques to check whether certain JavaScript functions are supported before executing them.
3. *Graceful Degradation*: Implement graceful degradation to ensure that essential website functions still work on browsers with limited JavaScript support.

Fixing Layout and Styling Issues

Layout and styling inconsistencies can occur due to differences in browser rendering engines.

Solution:

1. *Use CSS Resets*: Implement CSS resets to normalize browser styles and avoid unwanted style variations.
2. *Test Responsive Design*: Ensure that your website's responsive design works well across different screen sizes and devices.
3. *Browser-Specific CSS*: Use browser-specific CSS rules when necessary to address layout issues on specific browsers.

Addressing Browser-Specific Bugs and Quirks

Some browsers may have specific bugs or quirks that affect your website's performance.

Solution:

1. *Research Known Browser Issues*: Stay informed about known bugs and quirks of popular browsers and apply appropriate workarounds.
2. *Test Browser-Specific Code*: If you have browser-specific code or hacks, verify their effectiveness on target browsers.
3. *Use Conditional Comments*: Employ conditional comments or feature detection to serve browser-specific fixes only when needed.

Updating Browser Support for Outdated Browsers

Support for outdated browsers can hinder your website's performance and security.

Solution:

1. *Implement Browser Support Policies*: Establish clear browser support policies and communicate them to your website visitors.
2. *Encourage Browser Updates*: Display messages encouraging users to update their browsers to the latest versions for the best experience.
3. *Use Compatibility Libraries*: Consider using compatibility libraries or polyfills to add support for

modern features in older browsers.

Conclusion:

In conclusion, this chapter equips you with the expertise to solve browser compatibility problems effectively. By identifying compatibility issues, ensuring CSS and HTML standards compliance, handling JavaScript compatibility, fixing layout and styling issues, addressing browser-specific bugs and quirks, and updating browser support for outdated browsers, you'll be well-prepared to create a seamless and user-friendly website accessible across a wide range of browsers and devices. Browser compatibility is crucial for delivering a consistent user experience, and the insights gained from this chapter will empower you to approach browser compatibility troubleshooting with confidence and efficiency. As you continue your WordPress troubleshooting journey, the knowledge from this chapter will serve as a valuable resource to optimize your website's compatibility and enhance user satisfaction. Happy solving browser compatibility issues!

CHAPTER 26: HANDLING DNS AND DOMAIN ISSUES

In this critical chapter, we delve into the complexities of handling DNS and domain issues in WordPress and provide effective solutions to ensure your website's domain and DNS settings are configured correctly. DNS (Domain Name System) is a crucial component of web hosting that translates domain names into IP addresses, allowing visitors to access your website. However, misconfigured DNS settings, domain registration problems, and DNS propagation delays can lead to website inaccessibility and email delivery issues. By mastering the art of handling DNS and domain issues, you'll be empowered to maintain a stable and reliable online presence for your WordPress website.

Identifying DNS and Domain Issues
Before exploring solutions, it's crucial to identify the nature of DNS and domain issues affecting your WordPress website. Issues can range from DNS misconfigurations to expired domain registrations.

Solution:
1. ***Perform DNS Tests***: Utilize online DNS testing tools to check the health and accuracy of your website's DNS settings.
2. ***Monitor Domain Expiry***: Keep track of your domain's expiration date to prevent potential downtime due to expired registrations.
3. ***Check Registrar Information***: Verify that your domain

registrar's information is up-to-date and accurately reflects your contact details.

Troubleshooting DNS Misconfigurations
Incorrect DNS settings can lead to website inaccessibility and email delivery failures.

Solution:
1. *Double-Check DNS Records*: Review your DNS records, including A, CNAME, MX, and TXT records, to ensure they are properly configured.
2. *Use DNS Management Tools*: If using a third-party DNS management service, use their interface to review and modify DNS settings.
3. *Set Proper TTL Values*: Configure the Time-to-Live (TTL) values for DNS records appropriately to minimize propagation delays during updates.

Resolving Domain Registration Problems
Domain registration issues can disrupt your website's functionality and accessibility.

Solution:
1. *Verify Domain Ownership*: Ensure that you are the rightful owner of the domain and that your contact information is accurate in the domain registrar's records.
2. *Resolve Payment Issues*: If your domain registration is pending due to payment problems, address the issue with your domain registrar.
3. *Contact Domain Registrar Support*: If you encounter technical issues with domain registration, reach out to your domain registrar's support team for assistance.

Handling DNS Propagation Delays
DNS changes may take time to propagate globally, leading to temporary website inaccessibility.

Solution:

1. ***Monitor DNS Propagation***: Use online DNS propagation checkers to track the progress of DNS updates across different locations.
2. ***Be Patient***: DNS propagation delays are normal and can take up to 48 hours to complete. Be patient and allow time for changes to take effect.
3. ***Lower TTL Values***: Lower the TTL values of your DNS records before making changes to minimize propagation delays during updates.

Troubleshooting Email Delivery Problems

Email delivery issues can arise due to incorrect MX records or email server misconfigurations.

Solution:

1. ***Verify MX Records***: Confirm that your MX records point to the correct email servers responsible for handling incoming emails.
2. ***Check Email Server Configuration***: Review your email server settings and ensure that they comply with email delivery best practices.
3. ***Use Email Testing Tools***: Utilize email testing tools to simulate email delivery and detect potential problems.

Updating DNS for Website Migration

Website migration requires DNS updates to point to the new server or hosting provider.

Solution:

1. ***Prepare for Migration***: Plan and prepare for website migration by backing up your data and files.
2. ***Update DNS Records***: Update your DNS records to reflect the new IP address or nameservers of your new hosting provider.
3. ***Test Website Functionality***: After DNS updates, test your website thoroughly to ensure that it works

correctly on the new server.

Conclusion:

In conclusion, this chapter equips you with the expertise to handle DNS and domain issues effectively. By identifying DNS and domain issues, troubleshooting DNS misconfigurations, resolving domain registration problems, handling DNS propagation delays, troubleshooting email delivery problems, and updating DNS for website migration, you'll be well-prepared to maintain a stable and reliable online presence for your WordPress website. DNS and domain management are vital for website accessibility and email delivery, and the insights gained from this chapter will empower you to approach DNS and domain troubleshooting with confidence and efficiency. As you continue your WordPress troubleshooting journey, the knowledge from this chapter will serve as a valuable resource to optimize your DNS and domain settings and ensure a smooth and reliable website experience. Happy handling DNS and domain issues!

CHAPTER 27: TROUBLESHOOTING CROSS-BROWSER COMPATIBILITY

In this pivotal chapter, we address the complexities of troubleshooting cross-browser compatibility issues in WordPress and provide effective solutions to ensure your website functions seamlessly across various web browsers. Cross-browser compatibility is essential for delivering a consistent user experience to visitors using different browsers, devices, and operating systems. However, variations in browser rendering engines, support for web standards, and CSS compatibility can lead to layout problems and functionality discrepancies. By mastering the art of troubleshooting cross-browser compatibility, you'll be empowered to create a seamless and user-friendly website accessible to a broader audience.

Identifying Cross-Browser Compatibility Issues
Before exploring solutions, it's crucial to identify the nature of cross-browser compatibility issues on your WordPress website. Compatibility problems can manifest as layout discrepancies, broken functionalities, or design inconsistencies.

Solution:
1. *Perform Cross-Browser Testing*: Utilize cross-browser testing tools or online services to view your website across multiple browsers and versions.
2. *Monitor User Feedback*: Pay attention to user feedback and support requests related to browser-specific

issues.

3. **Conduct Regular Compatibility Checks**: Regularly conduct cross-browser compatibility checks to proactively identify and address potential issues.

Ensuring CSS and HTML Standards Compliance

CSS and HTML code that doesn't adhere to web standards can lead to browser rendering inconsistencies.

Solution:

1. **Use Valid CSS and HTML**: Ensure that your CSS and HTML code is valid and compliant with W3C web standards.
2. **Check Browser Prefixes**: Verify that any browser-specific CSS prefixes are correctly used to support different browser versions.
3. **Leverage CSS Frameworks**: Consider using CSS frameworks that have built-in cross-browser compatibility, such as Bootstrap or Foundation.

Handling JavaScript Compatibility

Browser variations in JavaScript support can cause functionality problems on your website.

Solution:

1. **Use Cross-Browser Compatible JavaScript Libraries**: Opt for widely used JavaScript libraries that have built-in cross-browser compatibility.
2. **Implement Feature Detection**: Use feature detection techniques to check whether certain JavaScript functions are supported before executing them.
3. **Provide Graceful Degradation**: Implement graceful degradation to ensure that essential website functions still work on browsers with limited JavaScript support.

Fixing Layout and Styling Inconsistencies

Layout and styling inconsistencies can occur due to differences in browser rendering engines.

Solution:

1. **Use CSS Resets**: Implement CSS resets to normalize browser styles and avoid unwanted style variations.
2. **Test Responsive Design**: Ensure that your website's responsive design works well across different screen sizes and devices.
3. **Leverage Browser-Specific CSS**: Use browser-specific CSS rules when necessary to address layout issues on specific browsers.

Addressing Browser-Specific Bugs and Quirks

Some browsers may have specific bugs or quirks that affect your website's performance.

Solution:

1. **Research Known Browser Issues**: Stay informed about known bugs and quirks of popular browsers and apply appropriate workarounds.
2. **Test Browser-Specific Code**: If you have browser-specific code or hacks, verify their effectiveness on target browsers.
3. **Use Conditional Comments**: Employ conditional comments or feature detection to serve browser-specific fixes only when needed.

Updating Browser Support for Outdated Versions

Support for outdated browser versions can hinder your website's performance and security.

Solution:

1. **Implement Browser Support Policies**: Establish clear browser support policies and communicate them to your website visitors.
2. **Encourage Browser Updates**: Display messages encouraging users to update their browsers to the latest versions for the best experience.
3. **Use Compatibility Libraries**: Consider using

compatibility libraries or polyfills to add support for modern features in older browsers.

Conclusion:

In conclusion, this chapter equips you with the expertise to troubleshoot cross-browser compatibility issues effectively. By identifying compatibility issues, ensuring CSS and HTML standards compliance, handling JavaScript compatibility, fixing layout and styling inconsistencies, addressing browser-specific bugs and quirks, and updating browser support for outdated versions, you'll be well-prepared to create a seamless and user-friendly website accessible across a wide range of browsers and devices. Cross-browser compatibility is crucial for delivering a consistent user experience, and the insights gained from this chapter will empower you to approach cross-browser compatibility troubleshooting with confidence and efficiency. As you continue your WordPress troubleshooting journey, the knowledge from this chapter will serve as a valuable resource to optimize your website's compatibility and enhance user satisfaction. Happy troubleshooting cross-browser compatibility!

CHAPTER 28: FIXING WORDPRESS MEMORY LIMIT ERRORS

In this critical chapter, we delve into the complexities of fixing WordPress memory limit errors and provide effective solutions to address memory-related issues on your WordPress website. Memory limit errors occur when your website exceeds the allocated PHP memory limit, leading to performance problems, plugin conflicts, and even the infamous "Fatal Error: Allowed Memory Size Exhausted" message. By mastering the art of fixing WordPress memory limit errors, you'll be empowered to optimize your website's memory usage, improve performance, and prevent potential crashes.

Identifying WordPress Memory Limit Errors
Before exploring solutions, it's crucial to identify the presence of memory limit errors on your WordPress website. Symptoms of memory limit issues may include slow loading times, white screens, or errors in the website's log files.

Solution:
1. ***Check Error Logs***: Review your website's error logs or server logs for any "memory exhausted" or PHP memory-related errors.
2. ***Monitor Website Performance***: Keep an eye on your website's performance, especially during peak traffic or plugin-heavy activities.
3. ***Use Debugging Tools***: Utilize debugging tools or

WordPress plugins to identify memory-intensive scripts or plugins.

Increasing PHP Memory Limit

One of the primary solutions to memory limit errors is increasing the PHP memory limit allocated to your website.

Solution:

1. *Modify php.ini File*: Access the php.ini file on your server and increase the memory_limit value. Contact your hosting provider if you're unsure how to access this file.
2. *Edit wp-config.php*: Alternatively, you can add the following code to your wp-config.php file to increase the memory limit: define('WP_MEMORY_LIMIT', '256M');
3. *Use .htaccess File*: If your server uses Apache, you can modify the .htaccess file with the following code: php_value memory_limit 256M.

Deactivating Memory-Intensive Plugins

Certain plugins can consume significant amounts of memory, leading to memory limit errors.

Solution:

1. *Identify Problematic Plugins*: Use debugging tools or the process of elimination to identify memory-intensive plugins.
2. *Deactivate and Replace*: Deactivate the identified plugins and find alternative plugins that offer similar functionality but with lower memory usage.
3. *Limit Plugin Usage*: Minimize the number of active plugins on your website to reduce the overall memory load.

Optimize Theme and Content

Inefficient themes and content structures can contribute to memory limit errors.

Solution:
1. *Choose Lightweight Themes*: Select lightweight and well-optimized themes that do not excessively consume server resources.
2. *Optimize Images*: Compress and resize images before uploading them to reduce their memory footprint.
3. *Use Excerpts*: Displaying excerpts instead of full content on archive pages can reduce the memory usage of your website.

Implement Caching and Performance Optimization

Caching mechanisms and performance optimization can reduce the need for excessive memory usage.

Solution:
1. *Use Caching Plugins*: Install and configure caching plugins to cache static content and reduce the load on your server.
2. *Enable Gzip Compression*: Enable Gzip compression to reduce the size of files sent from the server to the browser.
3. *Minify CSS and JavaScript*: Minify your CSS and JavaScript files to reduce their size and improve website performance.

Conclusion:

In conclusion, this chapter equips you with the expertise to fix WordPress memory limit errors effectively. By identifying memory limit errors, increasing PHP memory limits, deactivating memory-intensive plugins, optimizing themes and content, and implementing caching and performance optimization, you'll be well-prepared to optimize your website's memory usage, improve performance, and prevent potential crashes due to memory exhaustion. Memory limit errors are common challenges in WordPress, and the insights gained from this chapter will empower you to approach memory-related troubleshooting with confidence and efficiency. As you continue your WordPress troubleshooting journey, the knowledge from this chapter will serve as a valuable resource to ensure your website operates smoothly and efficiently, providing an enhanced user experience for your visitors. Happy fixing WordPress memory limit errors!

CHAPTER 29: RESOLVING "ERROR ESTABLISHING A DATABASE CONNECTION"

In this pivotal chapter, we address the critical issue of "Error Establishing a Database Connection" in WordPress and provide effective solutions to resolve this common problem. This error message occurs when WordPress is unable to connect to the database, resulting in a blank page or an error message on your website. The database is an essential component of WordPress, where all your website's content and settings are stored. Therefore, troubleshooting and resolving this issue promptly is crucial to restoring your website's functionality.

Identifying the Cause of the Error
Before exploring solutions, it's crucial to identify the root cause of the "Error Establishing a Database Connection" issue. The error can be triggered by various factors, including incorrect database credentials, database server issues, or a corrupted database.

Solution:
1. *Check Database Credentials*: Verify that the database username, password, and hostname in your wp-config.php file are correct.
2. *Test Database Connection*: Use database management tools or the PHP script to test whether you can connect to the database with the provided credentials.
3. *Verify Database Server Status*: Ensure that your

database server is running and accessible.

Fixing Incorrect Database Credentials

Incorrect or outdated database credentials can prevent WordPress from establishing a connection to the database.

Solution:

1. *Edit wp-config.php*: Open the wp-config.php file and update the database username, password, and hostname with the correct information provided by your hosting provider.
2. *Check Special Characters*: If your database password contains special characters, ensure they are correctly formatted and escaped in the wp-config.php file.
3. *Restore a Backup*: If you recently made changes to your wp-config.php file and are unsure about the correct credentials, restore a backup of the file from a working state.

Troubleshooting Database Server Issues

Issues with your database server can lead to connection problems with WordPress.

Solution:

1. *Check Database Server Status*: Confirm that your database server is running and accessible.
2. *Contact Your Hosting Provider*: If you're on shared hosting, reach out to your hosting provider to ensure there are no server-side issues affecting your database.
3. *Test Database Connection*: Use database management tools or the PHP script to test whether you can connect to the database server from a remote location.

Repairing a Corrupted Database

A corrupted database can cause connection errors and disrupt your website's functionality.

Solution:

1. *Use WordPress Repair Tool*: If you can access your WordPress dashboard, go to "Tools" > "Site Health" > "Database" and use the "Repair Database" feature.
2. *Restore Database Backup*: If you have a recent database backup, restore it to replace the corrupted database.
3. *Use phpMyAdmin*: If you have access to phpMyAdmin, run the "Repair" function on the corrupted database tables.

Optimize Database Performance

Optimizing your database can improve its performance and reduce the likelihood of connection errors.

Solution:

1. *Use a Database Optimization Plugin*: Install and use a reputable database optimization plugin to clean up and optimize your database tables.
2. *Delete Unnecessary Data*: Remove unnecessary plugins, themes, and content from your database to reduce its size and improve performance.
3. *Regular Backups*: Perform regular backups of your database to ensure you can restore it in case of any future issues.

Conclusion:

In conclusion, this chapter equips you with the expertise to resolve "Error Establishing a Database Connection" effectively. By identifying the cause of the error, fixing incorrect database credentials, troubleshooting database server issues, repairing a corrupted database, and optimizing database performance, you'll be well-prepared to restore your website's functionality and prevent future connection issues. The database is the backbone of your WordPress website, and the insights gained from this chapter will empower you to approach database-related troubleshooting with confidence and efficiency. As you continue your WordPress troubleshooting journey, the knowledge from this chapter will serve as a valuable resource to ensure the smooth and reliable operation of your website, delivering an enhanced user experience to your visitors. Happy resolving "Error Establishing a Database Connection"!

CHAPTER 30: TROUBLESHOOTING RSS FEED PROBLEMS

In this pivotal chapter, we explore the intricacies of troubleshooting RSS feed problems in WordPress and provide effective solutions to ensure your website's RSS feeds function smoothly. RSS (Really Simple Syndication) feeds are essential for distributing your website's content to subscribers and readers through feed readers or email subscriptions. However, issues with RSS feeds can result in broken or incomplete content distribution, affecting your website's visibility and engagement. By mastering the art of troubleshooting RSS feed problems, you'll be empowered to maintain a reliable content distribution mechanism and enhance your website's reach.

Identifying RSS Feed Issues
Before exploring solutions, it's crucial to identify the nature of RSS feed problems on your WordPress website. Symptoms may include broken feed links, missing content, or invalid feed errors.

Solution:
1. *Check Feed URL*: Verify that the URL of your RSS feed is correct and not affected by any permalink structure changes or plugin conflicts.
2. *Test Different Readers*: Test your RSS feed on various feed readers to identify whether the issue is specific to a particular reader or widespread.

3. *Monitor Feed Updates*: Keep an eye on the frequency and accuracy of your feed updates to identify any irregularities.

Resolving Invalid or Broken Feeds

Invalid or broken feeds can result from coding errors or conflicts with other plugins or themes.

Solution:

1. *Disable Recently Installed Plugins*: If the issue started after installing a new plugin, deactivate it temporarily to see if the problem resolves.
2. *Check Theme Compatibility*: Switch to a default WordPress theme temporarily to rule out any theme-related conflicts affecting the RSS feed.
3. *Validate Your Feed*: Use online RSS feed validation tools to identify and fix any coding errors in your feed.

Fixing Missing Content in Feeds

Content missing from your RSS feeds can result from content settings or incorrect template configurations.

Solution:

1. *Check Excerpt Settings*: Ensure that your RSS feed settings are configured to display the full content or a suitable excerpt of your posts.
2. *Examine Template Files*: Review your theme's template files (e.g., content.php, feed.php) to ensure they correctly handle content display in the feed.
3. *Regenerate Feed*: If your feed is missing recent content, try regenerating the feed using plugins or tools designed for this purpose.

Addressing Feed Update Frequency

Issues with feed update frequency can affect timely content distribution to subscribers.

Solution:

1. *Check Feed Update Settings*: Review your feed settings to ensure the update frequency is appropriate for your content publishing schedule.
2. *Use a Caching Plugin*: If your website uses caching plugins, consider excluding the RSS feeds from caching to ensure timely updates.
3. *Test Feed Update Speed*: Test the speed of your feed updates using various online tools to ensure timely delivery to subscribers.

Troubleshooting Feed URL Errors
Errors in your RSS feed URLs can lead to broken or invalid feeds.

Solution:
1. *Check Permalink Structure*: Ensure that your website's permalink structure is configured correctly and not causing conflicts with the feed URLs.
2. *Verify Feed URL Formats*: Confirm that your feed URLs are following the standard format (e.g., /feed/) and not altered by customizations.
3. *Use Redirects*: Implement 301 redirects for any incorrect or outdated feed URLs to the correct feed URL.

Conclusion:
In conclusion, this chapter equips you with the expertise to troubleshoot RSS feed problems effectively. By identifying RSS feed issues, resolving invalid or broken feeds, fixing missing content, addressing feed update frequency, and troubleshooting feed URL errors, you'll be well-prepared to maintain a reliable and seamless content distribution mechanism for your WordPress website. RSS feeds play a vital role in engaging readers and distributing your content, and the insights gained from this chapter will empower you to approach RSS feed troubleshooting with confidence and efficiency. As you continue your WordPress troubleshooting journey, the knowledge from this chapter will serve as a valuable resource to optimize your

website's RSS feeds and enhance content visibility and reach. Happy troubleshooting RSS feed problems!

CHAPTER 31: HANDLING WORDPRESS THEME CUSTOMIZATION ISSUES

In this crucial chapter, we delve into the intricacies of handling WordPress theme customization issues and provide effective solutions to ensure a seamless and visually appealing website customization experience. WordPress themes play a pivotal role in defining the look and feel of your website, but customization issues can arise due to misconfigurations, coding conflicts, or improper implementation. By mastering the art of handling WordPress theme customization issues, you'll be empowered to create a unique and personalized website that aligns perfectly with your brand and content.

Identifying Theme Customization Issues
Before exploring solutions, it's essential to identify the signs of theme customization issues on your WordPress website. Common indications may include broken layouts, missing customizations, or errors in custom code.

Solution:
1. ***Review Customization Settings***: If you encounter theme customization issues, review the customization settings in the WordPress Customizer or theme options panel to ensure they are correctly configured.
2. ***Check Theme Documentation***: Refer to your theme's documentation for guidelines on how to apply customizations and troubleshoot common issues.

Clearing Caches and Refreshing

Caching can sometimes affect the display of theme customizations, especially after updates.

Solution:

1. *Clear Browser Cache*: Instruct your users to clear their browser cache to ensure they are viewing the latest theme customizations.
2. *Refresh Customizer*: Use the "Refresh" button in the WordPress Customizer to update the live preview of your customizations.

Handling Custom Code Conflicts

Conflicts with custom code can lead to issues with theme customizations.

Solution:

1. *Isolate Custom Code*: Isolate the custom code used for theme customizations to identify if it's causing conflicts with other elements or plugins.
2. *Test Code on Staging Site*: Test custom code changes on a staging site before applying them to the live website to avoid disruptions.

Checking Responsive Design

Issues with responsive design can lead to inconsistencies in theme customizations across different devices.

Solution:

1. *Test on Multiple Devices*: Test your website on various devices (e.g., desktops, tablets, smartphones) to ensure theme customizations adapt appropriately to different screen sizes.
2. *Use Responsive-Friendly Plugins*: Employ responsive-friendly plugins to enhance the compatibility of customizations with different devices.

Verifying Browser Compatibility

Browser compatibility issues can affect the display of theme customizations.

Solution:
1. ***Test on Multiple Browsers***: Test your website on different browsers (e.g., Chrome, Firefox, Safari, Edge) to identify any inconsistencies in theme customizations.
2. **Use Browser Prefixes**: Apply browser prefixes in CSS for features that may require additional vendor-specific styling.

Reviewing Child Themes (If Applicable)
If using a child theme, issues may arise if the child theme is not set up correctly.

Solution:
1. ***Verify Child Theme Setup***: Check the child theme files and ensure they are correctly connected to the parent theme.
2. ***Check for Parent Theme Updates***: Confirm that both the parent and child themes are using the latest versions.

Conclusion:
In conclusion, this chapter equips you with the expertise to handle WordPress theme customization issues effectively. By identifying theme customization issues, clearing caches and refreshing, handling custom code conflicts, checking responsive design, verifying browser compatibility, and reviewing child themes (if applicable), you'll be well-prepared to create a visually stunning and personalized website that aligns perfectly with your vision. WordPress themes are essential for defining your website's aesthetics, and the insights gained from this chapter will empower you to approach theme customization troubleshooting with confidence and efficiency. As you continue your WordPress troubleshooting journey, the knowledge from this chapter will serve as a valuable resource to optimize

your theme customizations, prevent potential conflicts, and maintain a seamless and visually appealing WordPress website, ultimately contributing to a positive user experience and the long-term success of your online presence. Happy handling WordPress theme customization issues!

CHAPTER 32: FIXING WORDPRESS PAGINATION ISSUES

In this pivotal chapter, we delve into the complexities of fixing WordPress pagination issues and provide effective solutions to ensure smooth and accurate navigation of your website's content. Pagination is essential for organizing and presenting large sets of posts or pages, allowing visitors to browse through your content easily. However, pagination problems can lead to broken links, missing pages, or incorrect navigation, hampering user experience and website engagement. By mastering the art of fixing WordPress pagination issues, you'll be empowered to optimize your website's navigation and enhance user satisfaction.

Identifying Pagination Problems
Before exploring solutions, it's crucial to identify the nature of pagination issues on your WordPress website. Common problems may include broken page links, missing pagination, or incorrect page numbering.

<u>Solution</u>:
1. *Test Pagination on Different Browsers*: View your website's pagination on various browsers to check for cross-browser compatibility issues.
2. *Monitor Page URLs*: Verify that the page URLs in your pagination structure are correct and not affected by permalink settings or customizations.

3. *Check for Plugin Conflicts*: Deactivate plugins one by one to identify if any of them are causing pagination problems.

Fixing Broken Page Links

Broken links in pagination can result from incorrect permalinks or server configuration issues.

Solution:

1. *Update Permalink Structure*: Go to Settings > Permalinks in your WordPress dashboard and click "Save Changes" to update the permalink structure.
2. *Use Default Permalink Structure*: If custom permalink structures cause problems, switch to the default structure and test pagination.
3. *Check .htaccess File*: Verify that the .htaccess file in your WordPress root directory has the correct permissions and rewrite rules.

Restoring Missing Pagination

Missing pagination elements can occur due to coding errors or theme conflicts.

Solution:

1. *Review Template Files*: Inspect your theme's template files (e.g., archive.php, index.php) to ensure they include the necessary pagination code.
2. *Use Core WordPress Functions*: Utilize core WordPress functions like the_posts_pagination() or paginate_links() to generate pagination links.
3. *Check Theme Compatibility*: Switch to a default WordPress theme temporarily to check if the missing pagination is related to your current theme.

Correcting Incorrect Page Numbering

Incorrect page numbering can lead to navigation errors and frustrated visitors.

Solution:

1. ***Check Custom Queries***: If you use custom queries, ensure that they are set up correctly and do not affect the pagination order.
2. ***Reset Query***: Before generating pagination, use wp_reset_query() to reset the query and prevent interference with the pagination function.
3. ***Verify Posts per Page Setting***: Review your "Blog pages show at most" setting in Settings > Reading to ensure it matches your intended pagination.

Addressing Performance Issues

Large sets of content can cause slow-loading pagination, impacting user experience.

Solution:

1. ***Limit Queries***: Set the number of posts per page to an optimal value to reduce the load time of paginated content.
2. ***Use Caching***: Implement caching plugins to speed up the retrieval and display of paginated content.
3. ***Optimize Images and Media***: Compress and optimize images and media used in your paginated content to reduce loading times.

Conclusion:

In conclusion, this chapter equips you with the expertise to fix WordPress pagination issues effectively. By identifying pagination problems, fixing broken page links, restoring missing pagination, correcting incorrect page numbering, and addressing performance issues, you'll be well-prepared to optimize your website's navigation and enhance user satisfaction. Pagination is a crucial aspect of content organization, and the insights gained from this chapter will empower you to approach pagination troubleshooting with confidence and efficiency. As you continue your WordPress troubleshooting journey, the knowledge from this chapter will serve as a valuable resource to ensure smooth and accurate navigation of your website's content, creating a positive and engaging experience for your visitors. Happy fixing WordPress pagination issues!

CHAPTER 33: TROUBLESHOOTING SSL CERTIFICATE ERRORS

In this pivotal chapter, we explore the complexities of troubleshooting SSL certificate errors in WordPress and provide effective solutions to ensure a secure and error-free browsing experience for your website visitors. SSL certificates play a critical role in encrypting data transmitted between the user's browser and your website's server, providing a secure connection for sensitive information. However, SSL certificate errors can disrupt secure connections, leading to warning messages, insecure content, or potential data breaches. By mastering the art of troubleshooting SSL certificate errors, you'll be empowered to maintain a secure and trustworthy website environment.

Identifying SSL Certificate Errors
Before exploring solutions, it's crucial to identify the type of SSL certificate errors occurring on your WordPress website. Common SSL errors may include "SSL certificate not trusted," "SSL certificate expired," or "Mixed content" warnings.

Solution:
1. *Check Browser Warnings*: Inspect your website in various browsers to see if SSL certificate warning messages appear.
2. *SSL Certificate Details*: Review your SSL certificate details in your hosting provider's control panel to

check for expiration or misconfiguration.

3. *Monitor HTTPS Status*: Use online tools or browser extensions to check the HTTPS status of your website and potential mixed content issues.

Fixing SSL Certificate Trust Errors

SSL certificate trust errors occur when the certificate authority (CA) is not recognized or trusted by the user's browser.

Solution:

1. *Use Trusted CAs*: Obtain SSL certificates from reputable and recognized certificate authorities to ensure trust across all browsers.
2. *Install Intermediate Certificates*: If you receive trust errors, ensure that you have installed all necessary intermediate certificates provided by your CA.
3. **Update Root Certificates**: Ensure that your server's root certificate store is up-to-date to recognize the latest certificate authorities.

Resolving Expired SSL Certificates

Expired SSL certificates can cause severe security warnings and disrupt secure connections.

Solution:

1. *Renew SSL Certificate*: If your SSL certificate has expired, renew it through your hosting provider or certificate authority.
2. *Check Automatic Renewal*: Enable automatic SSL certificate renewal to avoid future expiration issues.
3. *Update Certificate Settings*: After renewing the certificate, update the SSL certificate settings on your server to reflect the new certificate.

Addressing Mixed Content Warnings

Mixed content warnings occur when your website contains a combination of secure (HTTPS) and insecure (HTTP) elements.

Solution:
1. ***Use Relative URLs***: Ensure that all URLs within your website's content (e.g., images, scripts) use relative URLs or HTTPS URLs.
2. ***Update Database Entries***: Use search and replace plugins or SQL queries to update database entries from HTTP to HTTPS.
3. ***Use Content Security Policy (CSP)***: Implement a Content Security Policy to enforce HTTPS content and prevent mixed content loading.

Troubleshooting Server Configuration Issues
Certain server configurations can cause SSL certificate errors.

Solution:
1. ***Check Server Software***: Verify that your server software (e.g., Apache, Nginx) is properly configured to support SSL/TLS connections.
2. ***Enable HTTPS***: Ensure that your server is set up to redirect all HTTP requests to HTTPS.
3. ***Verify Firewall Settings***: Check that your server's firewall settings do not interfere with SSL certificate communication.

Conclusion:
In conclusion, this chapter equips you with the expertise to troubleshoot SSL certificate errors effectively. By identifying SSL certificate errors, fixing trust errors, resolving expired certificates, addressing mixed content warnings, and troubleshooting server configuration issues, you'll be well-prepared to maintain a secure and error-free browsing experience for your WordPress website visitors. SSL certificates are crucial for data security and user trust, and the insights gained from this chapter will empower you to approach SSL certificate troubleshooting with confidence and efficiency. As you continue your WordPress troubleshooting journey, the

knowledge from this chapter will serve as a valuable resource to ensure a secure and trustworthy environment for your website users, fostering a positive and safe online experience. Happy troubleshooting SSL certificate errors!

CHAPTER 34: RESOLVING WORDPRESS MULTILINGUAL PLUGIN CONFLICTS

In this pivotal chapter, we delve into the intricacies of resolving WordPress multilingual plugin conflicts and provide effective solutions to ensure seamless multilingual functionality on your website. Multilingual plugins play a vital role in translating and presenting your website's content to diverse audiences. However, using multiple plugins or incompatible plugins can lead to conflicts, causing translation errors, broken layouts, or compromised user experience. By mastering the art of resolving WordPress multilingual plugin conflicts, you'll be empowered to create a harmonious multilingual environment that caters to your global audience.

Identifying Multilingual Plugin Conflicts
Before exploring solutions, it's crucial to identify the existence of conflicts between multilingual plugins on your WordPress website. Common signs may include untranslated content, broken translations, or clashes in language switchers.

Solution:
1. *Test Multilingual Features*: Check if all multilingual features, such as language switchers and translated content, are functioning as expected.
2. *Deactivate Plugins*: Temporarily deactivate one multilingual plugin at a time to see if the issue is resolved.

3. *Check Plugin Compatibility*: Ensure that your selected multilingual plugins are compatible with each other and with your theme.

Fixing Translation Discrepancies

Translation errors or missing translations can occur due to plugin incompatibilities or incorrect settings.

Solution:

1. *Check Translation Files*: Verify that your translation files are complete and correctly configured in each multilingual plugin.
2. *Use Translation Management*: Utilize translation management features of multilingual plugins to review and edit translations.
3. *Verify Content Synchronization*: Ensure that translated content is synchronized between different language versions.

Restoring Layout Consistency

Multilingual plugin conflicts can lead to layout inconsistencies or distorted elements.

Solution:

1. *Inspect Theme Compatibility*: Review your theme's compatibility with multilingual plugins, as certain themes may require specific configurations.
2. *Use Custom CSS*: Implement custom CSS to address layout conflicts between multilingual elements.
3. *Theme Update Check*: Check if your theme has any available updates that may resolve layout inconsistencies.

Resolving Language Switcher Issues

Issues with language switchers can affect user navigation and language selection.

Solution:

1. *Check Plugin Settings*: Review the settings of your language switcher plugin to ensure it is correctly configured.
2. *Use Theme-Specific Switchers*: If your theme provides built-in language switchers, consider using them for improved compatibility.
3. *Test Multiple Switchers*: Experiment with different language switcher plugins to find one that integrates seamlessly with your website.

Troubleshooting Performance Problems
Multiple multilingual plugins or conflicting settings can impact website performance.

Solution:
1. *Optimize Plugin Usage*: Limit the number of multilingual plugins to the ones you genuinely need, avoiding unnecessary overlap.
2. *Use Caching*: Implement caching plugins to optimize the loading time of translated content.
3. *Optimize Database Queries*: Review database queries related to multilingual plugins and optimize their performance.

Conclusion:
In conclusion, this chapter equips you with the expertise to resolve WordPress multilingual plugin conflicts effectively. By identifying multilingual plugin conflicts, fixing translation discrepancies, restoring layout consistency, resolving language switcher issues, and troubleshooting performance problems, you'll be well-prepared to create a seamless and user-friendly multilingual environment on your WordPress website. Multilingual plugins are instrumental in reaching a global audience, and the insights gained from this chapter will empower you to approach multilingual plugin conflicts with confidence and efficiency. As you continue your WordPress troubleshooting journey, the knowledge from this chapter

will serve as a valuable resource to create a harmonious and inclusive multilingual experience for your website users, fostering engagement and satisfaction across diverse linguistic backgrounds. Happy resolving WordPress multilingual plugin conflicts!

CHAPTER 35: FIXING WORDPRESS REST API ISSUES

In this pivotal chapter, we explore the complexities of fixing WordPress REST API issues and provide effective solutions to ensure seamless communication and data exchange between your website and external applications. The WordPress REST API allows developers to interact with your website's data programmatically, enabling the integration of various third-party services and applications. However, REST API issues can lead to authentication errors, data retrieval problems, or security vulnerabilities. By mastering the art of fixing WordPress REST API issues, you'll be empowered to unlock the full potential of your website's data and enhance its functionality.

Identifying REST API Problems
Before exploring solutions, it's crucial to identify the type of REST API issues occurring on your WordPress website. Common problems may include authentication failures, data retrieval errors, or incorrect API responses.

Solution:
1. *Enable Debugging*: Turn on WordPress debugging to view detailed error messages and identify REST API issues.
2. *Test API Endpoints*: Use tools like Postman or cURL to manually test API endpoints for response accuracy and

potential errors.

3. *Check Plugin Compatibility*: Ensure that your installed plugins do not interfere with the functionality of the REST API.

Fixing Authentication Errors

Authentication failures can occur when using incorrect credentials or encountering issues with authentication plugins.

Solution:

1. *Check API Keys*: Verify that you are using the correct API keys or tokens for authentication purposes.
2. *Reset Keys*: If you suspect a compromised key, reset your API keys and generate new ones for enhanced security.
3. *Review Authentication Plugins*: If you use authentication plugins, ensure they are configured correctly and not causing conflicts.

Resolving Data Retrieval Issues

Data retrieval problems may arise due to incorrect query parameters or server-side limitations.

Solution:

1. *Check Endpoint URL*: Review the endpoint URL and query parameters in your API requests for accuracy.
2. *Increase Server Resources*: If your website has large data sets or heavy queries, consider upgrading your server resources to support the data retrieval process.
3. *Optimize Queries*: Utilize query optimization techniques to enhance the efficiency of your API requests and data retrieval.

Addressing Incorrect API Responses

Incorrect API responses can be caused by faulty coding or data manipulation issues.

Solution:

1. *Validate Data Sources*: Ensure that the data sources used in API responses are reliable and up-to-date.
2. *Review Response Code*: Check the HTTP response codes in API requests to identify any underlying issues.
3. *Test Endpoint Output*: Manually test the output of API endpoints to verify the accuracy of the responses.

Handling REST API Security Vulnerabilities

Security vulnerabilities in the REST API can lead to unauthorized access or data breaches.

Solution:
1. *Use HTTPS*: Ensure that your website uses HTTPS to encrypt data transmitted via the REST API.
2. *Limit User Permissions*: Restrict user permissions to access sensitive API endpoints or data.
3. *Implement Authentication Checks*: Add additional authentication checks and validations to prevent unauthorized access.

Conclusion:

In conclusion, this chapter equips you with the expertise to fix WordPress REST API issues effectively. By identifying REST API problems, fixing authentication errors, resolving data retrieval issues, addressing incorrect API responses, and handling REST API security vulnerabilities, you'll be well-prepared to enable seamless communication and data exchange between your WordPress website and external applications. The WordPress REST API provides a powerful tool for developers, and the insights gained from this chapter will empower you to approach REST API troubleshooting with confidence and efficiency. As you continue your WordPress troubleshooting journey, the knowledge from this chapter will serve as a valuable resource to enhance your website's functionality and integration capabilities, fostering a more dynamic and connected digital presence. Happy fixing WordPress REST API issues!

CHAPTER 36: HANDLING WORDPRESS COMMENT SPAM

In this crucial chapter, we delve into the intricacies of handling WordPress comment spam and provide effective solutions to maintain a clean and engaging commenting environment on your website. Comment spam refers to the unsolicited and irrelevant comments left on your posts by bots or malicious users, often promoting unrelated links or products. These spam comments can clutter your website, diminish user experience, and potentially harm your website's reputation. By mastering the art of handling WordPress comment spam, you'll be empowered to maintain an interactive and spam-free commenting section that encourages genuine engagement and valuable discussions.

Identifying Comment Spam
Before exploring solutions, it's crucial to identify the signs of comment spam on your WordPress website. Common indications may include a large number of comments with irrelevant content, suspicious links, or repetitive messages.

Solution:
1. *Use Spam Filters*: Enable built-in comment spam filters or third-party anti-spam plugins to automatically detect and filter spam comments.
2. *Review Comments Regularly*: Regularly monitor your comments section and manually review suspicious

comments for potential spam.

3. *Check IP Addresses*: Identify and block suspicious IP addresses associated with spam comments.

Implementing CAPTCHA or reCAPTCHA

CAPTCHA and reCAPTCHA are powerful tools to distinguish between human users and automated bots, reducing spam submissions.

Solution:

1. *Enable CAPTCHA*: Add CAPTCHA challenges to your comment form to verify that the commenter is a human.
2. *Use reCAPTCHA v3*: Implement reCAPTCHA v3, which provides an invisible challenge and helps identify spam without user interaction.
3. *Adjust Sensitivity*: Fine-tune the sensitivity level of CAPTCHA or reCAPTCHA to strike a balance between spam protection and user convenience.

Enabling Comment Moderation

Comment moderation allows you to review and approve comments before they appear on your website.

Solution:

1. *Turn on Comment Moderation*: Enable comment moderation settings in WordPress to manually approve or disapprove comments.
2. *Set Keyword Filters*: Create keyword filters to automatically flag comments containing specific spam-related terms.
3. *Use Moderation Plugins*: Utilize comment moderation plugins to streamline the review process and enhance spam detection.

Disable HTML in Comments

Disabling HTML in comments prevents spam comments with malicious code or harmful links.

Solution:

1. *Use WordPress Settings*: In your WordPress discussion settings, disable HTML tags in comments.
2. *Implement Filtering*: Use custom filtering functions or plugins to remove HTML or specific HTML tags from comments.
3. *Sanitize User Inputs*: Apply data sanitization to comments to strip any potentially harmful code.

Limit Comment Links

Limiting the number of links allowed in comments helps prevent spam comments with excessive promotional or irrelevant links.

Solution:

1. *Set Link Limit*: Use plugins or custom functions to limit the number of links allowed per comment.
2. *Remove Excessive Links*: Manually review comments with an excessive number of links and remove or disapprove them.
3. *Educate Users*: Encourage users to limit the number of links they include in comments to maintain a spam-free environment.

Conclusion:

In conclusion, this chapter equips you with the expertise to handle WordPress comment spam effectively. By identifying comment spam, implementing CAPTCHA or reCAPTCHA, enabling comment moderation, disabling HTML in comments, and limiting comment links, you'll be well-prepared to maintain a clean and engaging commenting environment on your WordPress website. Comment sections provide valuable opportunities for user interaction and feedback, and the insights gained from this chapter will empower you to approach comment spam management with confidence and efficiency. As you continue your WordPress troubleshooting journey, the knowledge from this chapter will serve as a valuable resource to nurture meaningful discussions and foster a positive user experience, enhancing the overall engagement and credibility of your website. Happy handling WordPress comment spam!

CHAPTER 37: TROUBLESHOOTING BROKEN CONTACT FORMS

In this pivotal chapter, we explore the intricacies of troubleshooting broken contact forms on your WordPress website and provide effective solutions to ensure seamless communication with your visitors. Contact forms play a crucial role in enabling user interactions, inquiries, and feedback, but issues such as form submission failures, validation errors, or missing email notifications can disrupt this communication channel. By mastering the art of troubleshooting broken contact forms, you'll be empowered to maintain a reliable and functional contact form system that fosters engagement and enhances user satisfaction.

Identifying Contact Form Issues

Before exploring solutions, it's crucial to identify the type of problems occurring with your WordPress contact forms. Common issues may include form submission failures, error messages, or unresponsive form fields.

Solution:

1. ***Test Form Submissions***: Manually test your contact form to check for any errors or failures during the submission process.
2. ***Review Error Messages***: Analyze any error messages or notifications displayed when users submit the form.
3. ***Check Form Settings***: Verify that the form settings and

configurations are correctly set up in your contact form plugin.

Fixing Form Validation Errors

Form validation errors can occur when users fail to provide required information or when incorrect data formats are submitted.

<u>Solution</u>:

1. *Review Form Fields*: Ensure that all required fields are clearly marked, and the validation rules are set correctly.
2. *Customize Error Messages*: Use custom error messages to guide users in providing the correct information.
3. *Test Form Validation*: Manually test different form scenarios to identify any validation errors and resolve them.

Restoring Email Notifications

Missing email notifications can lead to overlooked inquiries and missed opportunities.

<u>Solution</u>:

1. *Check Email Settings*: Review the email settings in your contact form plugin to ensure that email notifications are enabled and correctly configured.
2. *Test Email Delivery*: Use the email test functionality in your contact form plugin to verify if emails are being delivered successfully.
3. *Monitor Spam Filters*: Check your spam filters or email provider's settings to ensure that email notifications are not mistakenly flagged as spam.

Resolving Form Submission Failures

Form submission failures can result from server issues or conflicts with other plugins.

<u>Solution</u>:

1. *Verify Server Compatibility*: Check if your server environment meets the requirements of your contact form plugin.
2. *Test Conflict with Plugins*: Temporarily deactivate other plugins and test the contact form to identify any conflicts affecting form submissions.
3. *Check Form Routing*: Ensure that the form submissions are correctly routed to the designated email addresses or databases.

Troubleshooting AJAX Errors
AJAX-related errors can affect the smooth functionality of contact forms.

Solution:
1. *Check AJAX Requests*: Inspect AJAX requests made by your contact form and verify if they are returning the correct responses.
2. *Debug AJAX Functions*: Use WordPress debugging tools to identify and resolve any AJAX-related issues.
3. *Update JavaScript Libraries*: Ensure that your contact form's JavaScript libraries are up-to-date and compatible with your WordPress version.

Conclusion:
In conclusion, this chapter equips you with the expertise to troubleshoot broken contact forms effectively. By identifying contact form issues, fixing form validation errors, restoring email notifications, resolving form submission failures, and troubleshooting AJAX errors, you'll be well-prepared to maintain a reliable and functional contact form system on your WordPress website. Contact forms serve as an essential communication channel with your visitors, and the insights gained from this chapter will empower you to approach contact form troubleshooting with confidence and efficiency. As you continue your WordPress troubleshooting journey, the knowledge from this chapter will serve as a valuable resource

to enhance user interactions, inquiries, and feedback, fostering engagement and strengthening the connection with your audience. Happy troubleshooting broken contact forms!

CHAPTER 38: ADDRESSING WORDPRESS XML-RPC ISSUES

In this pivotal chapter, we delve into the complexities of addressing WordPress XML-RPC issues and provide effective solutions to ensure secure and reliable communication between your WordPress site and external applications or services. XML-RPC (XML Remote Procedure Call) is a protocol that allows remote access to WordPress functionalities, enabling third-party apps, plugins, or platforms to interact with your site's data. However, XML-RPC issues can lead to security vulnerabilities, performance problems, or connection errors. By mastering the art of addressing WordPress XML-RPC issues, you'll be empowered to optimize your site's XML-RPC functionality and enhance its overall performance.

Identifying XML-RPC Issues

Before exploring solutions, it's crucial to identify the signs of XML-RPC issues on your WordPress website. Common indications may include connection errors with external apps, security warnings, or slow performance.

Solution:

1. ***Check Server Logs***: Inspect your server logs for any XML-RPC-related errors or connection issues.
2. ***Test External Apps***: Manually test the communication between your WordPress site and external apps that rely on XML-RPC.

3. *Use XML-RPC Debugging*: Enable XML-RPC debugging in WordPress to view detailed information about XML-RPC requests and responses.

Enhancing XML-RPC Security

XML-RPC can be exploited by malicious users to perform brute force attacks or unauthorized actions.

Solution:

1. *Disable XML-RPC*: If you don't use XML-RPC functionality, consider disabling it to reduce the attack surface.
2. *Use Plugins for Security*: Implement security plugins that offer XML-RPC protection and limit access to authorized users.
3. *Enable Two-Factor Authentication*: Require two-factor authentication for XML-RPC requests to add an extra layer of security.

Optimizing XML-RPC Performance

XML-RPC requests can impact your site's performance, especially during high-traffic periods.

Solution:

1. *Limit XML-RPC Requests*: Minimize the number of XML-RPC requests made to your WordPress site.
2. *Optimize Server Resources*: Upgrade your server resources to handle XML-RPC requests more efficiently.
3. *Use Caching*: Implement caching mechanisms to reduce the load caused by repeated XML-RPC requests.

Resolving Connection Errors

XML-RPC connection errors can occur due to server misconfigurations or firewall restrictions.

Solution:

1. *Check Firewall Settings*: Review your server's firewall settings to ensure they allow XML-RPC requests.

2. *Verify Server Configurations*: Check if your server is correctly configured to handle XML-RPC communication.
3. *Test Different Devices*: Try accessing your WordPress site through different devices to check for connection errors.

Troubleshooting XML-RPC Plugin Conflicts
Certain plugins might conflict with XML-RPC functionality, leading to errors or unexpected behavior.

Solution:

1. *Deactivate Plugins*: Temporarily deactivate other plugins and test XML-RPC functionality to identify conflicts.
2. *Update Plugins*: Ensure that all plugins are up-to-date to minimize compatibility issues with XML-RPC.
3. *Verify Plugin Compatibility*: Review the compatibility of your plugins with XML-RPC and adjust settings if needed.

Conclusion:
In conclusion, this chapter equips you with the expertise to address WordPress XML-RPC issues effectively. By identifying XML-RPC issues, enhancing XML-RPC security, optimizing performance, resolving connection errors, and troubleshooting plugin conflicts, you'll be well-prepared to ensure secure and reliable communication between your WordPress site and external applications. XML-RPC is a powerful tool for remote access to WordPress functionalities, and the insights gained from this chapter will empower you to approach XML-RPC troubleshooting with confidence and efficiency. As you continue your WordPress troubleshooting journey, the knowledge from this chapter will serve as a valuable resource to optimize XML-RPC functionality, enhance security, and foster seamless communication with third-party apps or services, enriching the overall user experience and expanding the capabilities of your

WordPress site. Happy addressing WordPress XML-RPC issues!

CHAPTER 39: SOLVING WORDPRESS PERMALINK PROBLEMS

In this pivotal chapter, we explore the intricacies of solving WordPress permalink problems and provide effective solutions to ensure clean, user-friendly, and search engine-friendly URLs on your website. Permalinks are the permanent URLs that point to your individual posts, pages, or custom content on WordPress. However, issues such as broken permalinks, 404 errors, or improper URL structures can affect your website's SEO, user experience, and navigation. By mastering the art of solving WordPress permalink problems, you'll be empowered to maintain an optimized permalink structure that enhances your website's overall accessibility and visibility.

Identifying Permalink Issues
Before exploring solutions, it's crucial to identify the signs of permalink problems on your WordPress website. Common indications may include broken links, 404 error pages, or URLs not reflecting your preferred structure.

Solution:
1. *Test Permalinks*: Manually test the permalinks of your posts, pages, and custom content to check for broken links or errors.
2. *Review Server Configurations*: Ensure that your server environment supports the permalink structure you want to use.

3. *Use WordPress Debugging*: Enable WordPress debugging to view any permalink-related errors or warnings.

Fixing Broken Permalinks

Broken permalinks can occur when posts or pages are moved, deleted, or when the permalink structure is changed.

Solution:

1. *Update Permalink Structure*: Adjust the permalink structure in WordPress settings to match your desired URL format.
2. *Use Redirection Plugin*: Implement a redirection plugin to automatically redirect old permalinks to their new locations.
3. *Manually Fix Links*: Review your content and manually update internal links to point to the correct permalinks.

Resolving 404 Error Pages

404 errors can result from incorrect permalinks or issues with the server.

Solution:

1. *Reset Permalinks*: Go to WordPress settings and reset the permalinks to their default settings, then set them back to your preferred structure.
2. *Check .htaccess File*: Verify that the .htaccess file in your WordPress root directory is writable and contains the correct permalink rules.
3. *Regenerate .htaccess File*: If the .htaccess file is missing or corrupted, regenerate it using WordPress' built-in function.

Improving URL Structure for SEO

A well-structured URL can positively impact your website's search engine rankings.

Solution:

1. *Use Descriptive URLs*: Create descriptive and keyword-rich URLs that accurately reflect the content of your posts and pages.
2. *Remove Stop Words*: Avoid using unnecessary stop words (e.g., "and," "the," "of") in your permalinks.
3. *Implement Hyphens*: Use hyphens to separate words in your URLs for better readability and SEO.

Handling Permalinks for Custom Post Types
Custom post types may require specific permalink structures or adjustments.

Solution:

1. *Check Custom Post Type Settings*: Review the settings of your custom post types to ensure they have the desired permalink structure.
2. *Update Rewrite Rules*: If needed, modify rewrite rules for custom post types to match your preferred URL format.
3. *Regenerate Permalinks*: After making changes to custom post type settings, regenerate permalinks to apply the updates.

Conclusion:
In conclusion, this chapter equips you with the expertise to solve WordPress permalink problems effectively. By identifying permalink issues, fixing broken permalinks, resolving 404 error pages, improving URL structure for SEO, and handling permalinks for custom post types, you'll be well-prepared to maintain clean, user-friendly, and search engine-friendly URLs on your WordPress website. Permalinks are vital for both user navigation and SEO, and the insights gained from this chapter will empower you to approach permalink troubleshooting with confidence and efficiency. As you continue your WordPress troubleshooting journey, the knowledge from this chapter

will serve as a valuable resource to optimize your permalink structure, enhance your website's accessibility, and boost its visibility in search engine results, ultimately fostering a more enjoyable and rewarding user experience. Happy solving WordPress permalink problems!

CHAPTER 40: RESOLVING SERVER CONFIGURATION ISSUES

In this pivotal chapter, we explore the complexities of resolving server configuration issues on your WordPress website and provide effective solutions to ensure optimal performance, security, and stability. The server configuration is a crucial component that directly impacts how your WordPress site functions and interacts with various resources. However, misconfigurations, compatibility problems, or resource limitations can lead to various website issues, such as errors, slow loading times, or even downtime. By mastering the art of resolving server configuration issues, you'll be empowered to fine-tune your server settings and ensure a smooth and reliable operation of your WordPress site.

Identifying Server Configuration Problems
Before exploring solutions, it's crucial to identify signs of server configuration issues on your WordPress website. Common indications may include 500 internal server errors, slow page loading, or plugin conflicts.

Solution:
1. *Review Error Logs*: Inspect your server's error logs to identify any recurring issues or error messages related to server configuration.
2. *Monitor Resource Usage*: Use server monitoring tools to keep track of CPU, memory, and disk usage to identify

resource limitations.

3. *Test Plugin Compatibility*: Temporarily deactivate plugins to check if any are causing conflicts due to server configuration discrepancies.

Resolving 500 Internal Server Errors

The 500 internal server error is a generic error indicating a problem on the server side.

Solution:

1. *Check .htaccess File*: Ensure the .htaccess file in your WordPress root directory doesn't contain any conflicting rules.
2. *Verify File Permissions*: Review file and folder permissions on your server to ensure they are correctly set.
3. *Increase PHP Memory Limit*: If your website's PHP memory limit is low, increase it to avoid 500 errors caused by insufficient memory.

Optimizing Server Performance

Server performance issues can lead to slow page loading times and a poor user experience.

Solution:

1. *Enable Caching*: Implement caching mechanisms, such as browser caching or server-side caching, to reduce server load and speed up page loading times.
2. *Utilize Content Delivery Networks (CDNs)*: Offload static content to CDNs to distribute assets geographically and reduce server response times.
3. *Optimize Database Queries*: Review and optimize database queries to enhance server performance during database interactions.

Handling Resource Limitations

Resource limitations, such as CPU or memory restrictions, can affect your site's responsiveness and scalability.

Solution:

1. ***Upgrade Hosting Plan***: If your current hosting plan doesn't provide sufficient resources, consider upgrading to a higher-tier plan.
2. ***Optimize Themes and Plugins***: Use lightweight and well-coded themes and plugins to minimize resource usage.
3. ***Monitor Resource Usage***: Regularly monitor your server's resource usage and proactively address potential bottlenecks.

Securing Your Server

Server security is critical to safeguarding your WordPress site from potential threats.

Solution:

1. ***Install SSL Certificate***: Implement an SSL certificate to encrypt data transmitted between your server and users' browsers.
2. ***Enable Firewall Protection***: Set up a firewall to block unauthorized access and prevent malicious attacks.
3. ***Update Software Regularly***: Keep your server's operating system, web server, and other software up-to-date to patch security vulnerabilities.

Conclusion:

In conclusion, this chapter equips you with the expertise to resolve server configuration issues effectively. By identifying server configuration problems, resolving 500 internal server errors, optimizing server performance, handling resource limitations, and securing your server, you'll be well-prepared to fine-tune your server settings and ensure a smooth and reliable operation of your WordPress site. The server configuration is a crucial pillar for your website's performance and security, and the insights gained from this chapter will empower you to approach server troubleshooting with confidence and efficiency. As you continue your WordPress troubleshooting journey, the knowledge from this chapter will serve as a valuable resource to optimize your server environment, enhance your website's performance, and strengthen its defenses against potential threats, ultimately contributing to an exceptional user experience and a flourishing digital presence. Happy resolving server configuration issues!

CHAPTER 41: FIXING WORDPRESS RSS FEED ERRORS

In this essential chapter, we explore the intricacies of fixing WordPress RSS feed errors and provide effective solutions to ensure the seamless generation and distribution of your website's content to subscribers and feed readers. RSS (Really Simple Syndication) feeds play a crucial role in delivering your posts, updates, and news to users and external platforms. However, issues such as invalid XML, missing feed items, or broken feed URLs can disrupt the RSS feed functionality and prevent content dissemination. By mastering the art of fixing WordPress RSS feed errors, you'll be empowered to maintain a reliable and well-functioning RSS feed system that keeps your audience informed and engaged.

Identifying RSS Feed Issues

Before exploring solutions, it's crucial to identify signs of RSS feed errors on your WordPress website. Common indications may include blank or incomplete feed content, "XML Parsing Error" messages, or issues with feed readers.

Solution:

1. *Test Feed URLs*: Manually check your RSS feed URLs to ensure they are working and generating the correct content.
2. *Use Feed Validation Tools*: Utilize online RSS feed validation tools to identify any XML errors or invalid

feed formats.
3. *Check Feed Readers*: Verify that your RSS feed readers or third-party platforms can access and display your RSS feeds correctly.

Fixing Invalid XML Errors

Invalid XML errors can occur when your RSS feed contains incorrect or malformed XML code.

Solution:
1. *Check Content Formatting*: Ensure that your posts and content are correctly formatted to comply with XML standards.
2. *Use Plugins for Validation*: Implement WordPress plugins that validate your RSS feeds and automatically fix XML errors.
3. *Verify Special Characters*: Check for any special characters or symbols that might be causing XML parsing errors.

Resolving Missing Feed Items

Missing feed items can happen if there are unpublished or private posts that should not appear in the RSS feed.

Solution:
1. *Exclude Unpublished Posts*: Use plugins or settings in your RSS feed to exclude unpublished or private posts from the feed.
2. *Check Post Visibility*: Review the visibility settings of your posts to ensure they are public and should be included in the RSS feed.
3. *Regenerate Feed*: If necessary, regenerate the RSS feed to ensure all relevant and published content is included.

Handling Broken Feed URLs

Broken feed URLs can result from incorrect server configurations or permalink issues.

Solution:

1. **Verify Permalink Settings**: Check your WordPress permalink settings to ensure they are correctly configured and not causing broken feed URLs.
2. **Reset Permalinks**: If you recently made changes to your permalink structure, reset them to the default settings and then set them back to your preferred structure.
3. **Test Feed URL Accessibility**: Manually access your feed URLs to check for any server or access issues.

Troubleshooting Plugin Conflicts

Certain plugins might conflict with RSS feed functionality, leading to errors or unexpected behavior.

Solution:

1. **Deactivate Plugins**: Temporarily deactivate other plugins and test the RSS feed to identify conflicts caused by plugin discrepancies.
2. **Update Plugins**: Ensure that all plugins are up-to-date to minimize compatibility issues with RSS feeds.
3. **Verify Plugin Compatibility**: Review the compatibility of your plugins with RSS feed functionality and adjust settings if needed.

Conclusion:

In conclusion, this chapter equips you with the expertise to fix WordPress RSS feed errors effectively. By identifying RSS feed issues, fixing invalid XML errors, resolving missing feed items, handling broken feed URLs, and troubleshooting plugin conflicts, you'll be well-prepared to maintain a reliable and well-functioning RSS feed system on your WordPress website. RSS feeds are crucial for content dissemination and audience engagement, and the insights gained from this chapter will empower you to approach RSS feed troubleshooting with confidence and efficiency. As you continue your WordPress troubleshooting journey, the knowledge from this chapter will serve as a valuable resource to keep your audience informed, boost content distribution, and foster continuous engagement, ultimately contributing to the growth and success of your WordPress site. Happy fixing WordPress RSS feed errors!

CHAPTER 42: TROUBLESHOOTING WORDPRESS CRON JOB PROBLEMS

In this crucial chapter, we explore the complexities of troubleshooting WordPress cron job problems and provide effective solutions to ensure the timely execution of scheduled tasks on your website. Cron jobs are essential for automating various WordPress processes, such as publishing scheduled posts, checking for updates, or running plugin tasks. However, issues such as missed or delayed cron jobs, misconfigurations, or conflicts with other plugins can disrupt the proper functioning of scheduled tasks. By mastering the art of troubleshooting WordPress cron job problems, you'll be empowered to maintain a reliable and efficient cron job system that keeps your WordPress site running smoothly.

Identifying Cron Job Issues

Before exploring solutions, it's crucial to identify the signs of cron job problems on your WordPress website. Common indications may include missed scheduled posts, outdated data, or errors in plugin functionalities that rely on cron jobs.

Solution:

1. *Check Scheduled Tasks*: Manually verify the execution of scheduled tasks, such as publishing posts, to

determine if cron jobs are functioning correctly.

2. ***Monitor Cron Job Logs***: Inspect cron job logs to identify any errors or delays in the execution of scheduled tasks.

3. ***Test Plugin Functionality***: Temporarily deactivate plugins that rely on cron jobs to check if they are causing any conflicts.

Resolving Missed or Delayed Cron Jobs

Missed or delayed cron jobs can occur due to server restrictions or traffic spikes.

Solution:

1. ***Set Up External Cron***: Configure an external cron job using your hosting provider's control panel to ensure more reliable and timely execution of cron tasks.

2. ***Use Cron Management Plugins***: Implement WordPress plugins that optimize cron job handling and help prevent missed or delayed tasks.

3. ***Adjust Cron Intervals***: Modify the intervals for specific cron jobs to better match your website's traffic patterns and server resources.

Handling Misconfigured Cron Jobs

Misconfigurations in cron job settings can lead to execution failures or unexpected results.

Solution:

1. ***Verify WP-Cron Configuration***: Check if your website's WP-Cron is correctly enabled and functioning.

2. ***Adjust Server Timezone***: Ensure that your server's timezone settings match your WordPress website's timezone.

3. ***Review Plugin Settings***: Inspect the settings of plugins using cron jobs to confirm that they are properly configured.

Troubleshooting Cron Job Conflicts

Cron job conflicts with other plugins or server tasks can result in errors or hinder the smooth execution of tasks.

Solution:

1. *Check Plugin Interactions*: Test plugins individually and identify if any are causing conflicts with cron jobs.
2. *Adjust Cron Job Order*: Modify the execution order of cron jobs to avoid conflicts between tasks.
3. *Limit Resource Usage*: Optimize the resource usage of cron jobs to prevent conflicts with other server tasks.

Verifying Email Notifications

Email notifications for cron job tasks can help you monitor their execution and identify potential issues.

Solution:

1. *Test Email Delivery*: Ensure that your WordPress site can send email notifications for successful and failed cron jobs.
2. *Use Logging Plugins*: Implement logging plugins that provide detailed records of cron job executions and email notifications.
3. *Monitor Email Responses*: Regularly check your email inbox for cron job notifications to stay informed about their status.

Conclusion:

In conclusion, this chapter equips you with the expertise to troubleshoot WordPress cron job problems effectively. By identifying cron job issues, resolving missed or delayed cron jobs, handling misconfigurations, troubleshooting conflicts, and verifying email notifications, you'll be well-prepared to maintain a reliable and efficient cron job system on your WordPress website. Cron jobs are essential for automating various tasks and processes, and the insights gained from this chapter will empower you to approach cron job troubleshooting with confidence and efficiency. As you continue your WordPress troubleshooting journey, the knowledge from this chapter will serve as a valuable resource to optimize your cron job setup, enhance task automation, and ensure the smooth functioning of scheduled tasks, ultimately contributing to a streamlined and well-organized WordPress site. Happy troubleshooting WordPress cron job problems!

CHAPTER 43: HANDLING WORDPRESS DASHBOARD ERRORS

In this critical chapter, we delve into the intricacies of handling WordPress dashboard errors and provide effective solutions to ensure smooth and efficient management of your website's backend. The WordPress dashboard serves as the control center for website administrators, allowing them to create, edit, and manage content, plugins, and settings. However, issues such as blank or inaccessible dashboards, error messages, or missing features can disrupt your ability to perform essential tasks. By mastering the art of handling WordPress dashboard errors, you'll be empowered to maintain a functional and user-friendly dashboard that facilitates seamless website administration.

Identifying Dashboard Issues

Before exploring solutions, it's crucial to identify the signs of dashboard errors on your WordPress website. Common indications may include a blank or partially loaded dashboard, error messages, or missing admin menu items.

Solution:

1. ***Check Browser Compatibility***: Test your WordPress dashboard in different browsers to rule out browser-specific issues.
2. ***Review Error Messages***: Inspect any error messages displayed on the dashboard to identify the specific nature of the problem.

3. *Disable Plugins*: Temporarily deactivate plugins to check if any are causing conflicts or interfering with dashboard functionality.

Resolving Blank Dashboard or White Screen Errors

A blank dashboard or white screen can occur due to PHP errors, memory limitations, or theme conflicts.

Solution:

1. *Enable Debugging*: Turn on WordPress debugging to view any PHP errors that might be causing the blank dashboard.
2. *Increase PHP Memory Limit*: Increase the PHP memory limit in your server settings to ensure your dashboard has enough resources to load properly.
3. *Switch to Default Theme*: Temporarily switch to a default WordPress theme to check if the issue is caused by a theme conflict.

Fixing Plugin Conflicts

Certain plugins might conflict with the dashboard's functionality, leading to errors or missing features.

Solution:

1. *Disable Plugins*: Deactivate plugins one by one to identify the plugin causing the conflict and resolve the issue accordingly.
2. *Update Plugins*: Ensure all plugins are up-to-date to minimize compatibility issues with the WordPress dashboard.
3. *Verify Plugin Compatibility*: Check the compatibility of your plugins with the latest version of WordPress and adjust settings if needed.

Handling Missing Admin Menu Items

Missing admin menu items can happen due to user roles, plugin settings, or database issues.

Solution:
1. **Check User Roles**: Review user roles and permissions to ensure the affected users have access to the missing admin menu items.
2. **Reset Plugin Settings**: If the issue is caused by a plugin, reset its settings to the default configuration and reconfigure as needed.
3. **Repair Database**: Use the WordPress database repair tool to fix any database-related problems that may be affecting the admin menu.

Resolving HTTP Error 500 in the Dashboard
An HTTP error 500 in the dashboard typically indicates a server-side problem.

Solution:
1. **Check .htaccess File**: Verify the .htaccess file in your WordPress root directory for any incorrect configurations.
2. **Review Server Logs**: Inspect your server logs for any critical errors that might shed light on the cause of the HTTP error 500.
3. **Contact Hosting Support**: If the issue persists, contact your hosting provider's support team for assistance in resolving server-related problems.

Conclusion:
In conclusion, this chapter equips you with the expertise to handle WordPress dashboard errors effectively. By identifying dashboard issues, resolving blank dashboard or white screen errors, fixing plugin conflicts, handling missing admin menu items, and resolving HTTP error 500, you'll be well-prepared to maintain a functional and user-friendly dashboard on your WordPress website. The WordPress dashboard is a vital component for website administration, and the insights gained from this chapter will empower you to approach dashboard

error troubleshooting with confidence and efficiency. As you continue your WordPress troubleshooting journey, the knowledge from this chapter will serve as a valuable resource to ensure a smooth and efficient backend management experience, ultimately contributing to a streamlined and successful WordPress site. Happy handling WordPress dashboard errors!

CHAPTER 44: RESOLVING WORDPRESS WIDGET ISSUES

In this crucial chapter, we explore the complexities of resolving WordPress widget issues and provide effective solutions to ensure the seamless functioning and display of widgets on your website. Widgets play a significant role in customizing and enhancing various aspects of your website's layout and functionality, such as sidebars, footers, or custom widget areas. However, issues such as missing or malfunctioning widgets, layout inconsistencies, or conflicts with themes or plugins can hinder the optimal presentation of your website's content. By mastering the art of resolving WordPress widget issues, you'll be empowered to maintain a visually appealing and highly functional widget system that complements your website's design.

Identifying Widget Problems

Before exploring solutions, it's crucial to identify the signs of widget issues on your WordPress website. Common indications may include missing widgets, layout misalignments, or error messages.

Solution:

1. *Review Widget Settings*: Inspect the widget settings in the WordPress dashboard to ensure they are configured correctly.
2. *Test Widget Display*: Manually test each widget's display in different areas of your website to pinpoint any specific issues

3. *Check Theme Compatibility*: Verify if the current theme supports the widgets you are using and if any conflicts arise.

Fixing Missing or Unavailable Widgets

Missing widgets can occur due to plugin conflicts, theme updates, or database issues.

Solution:
1. *Deactivate Conflicting Plugins*: Temporarily deactivate plugins to identify if any are causing conflicts and preventing widgets from displaying.
2. *Update Themes and Plugins*: Ensure that both your theme and plugins are up-to-date to maintain compatibility and resolve any widget-related issues.
3. *Regenerate Widgets*: If a widget has disappeared from the widget area, try re-adding it to restore its display.

Resolving Widget Layout Inconsistencies

Widget layout inconsistencies may arise due to CSS conflicts or responsive design issues.

Solution:
1. *Inspect CSS Styles*: Review your website's CSS styles to identify any conflicts that might be affecting widget layout.
2. *Use CSS Specificity*: Adjust the CSS specificity of your widget styles to ensure they take precedence over conflicting styles.
3. *Optimize Responsive Design*: Optimize your widget styles for responsiveness to ensure a consistent layout across different devices.

Handling Widget Display Errors

Widget display errors can result from coding issues or plugin conflicts.

Solution:

1. *Check PHP Errors*: Enable WordPress debugging to view any PHP errors that might be affecting widget display.
2. *Disable JavaScript Minification*: If you use a caching or optimization plugin with JavaScript minification, try disabling it to see if it resolves widget display errors.
3. *Test Widget in Isolation*: Remove widgets one by one to identify if a specific widget is causing the display error.

Troubleshooting Widget Functionality
Widget functionality issues may arise due to plugin conflicts or custom code discrepancies.

Solution:
1. *Use Plugin Compatibility*: Choose widgets and plugins from reputable sources and ensure they are compatible with your current WordPress version.
2. *Check Plugin Settings*: Review the settings of plugins that affect widget functionality to ensure they are configured correctly.
3. *Verify Custom Code*: If you have custom code affecting widgets, verify that it aligns with WordPress coding standards and doesn't interfere with widget functionality.

Conclusion:
In conclusion, this chapter equips you with the expertise to resolve WordPress widget issues effectively. By identifying widget problems, fixing missing or unavailable widgets, resolving layout inconsistencies, handling widget display errors, and troubleshooting widget functionality, you'll be well-prepared to maintain a visually appealing and highly functional widget system on your WordPress website. Widgets are essential for customizing your website's appearance and enhancing its user experience, and the insights gained from this chapter will empower you to approach widget troubleshooting with confidence and efficiency. As you continue your WordPress troubleshooting journey, the knowledge from this chapter will

serve as a valuable resource to optimize your widget setup, ensure smooth widget functionality, and present a polished and engaging user interface, ultimately contributing to an exceptional and user-friendly WordPress site. Happy resolving WordPress widget issues!

CHAPTER 45: FIXING WORDPRESS CUSTOM POST TYPE PROBLEMS

In this essential chapter, we explore the intricacies of fixing WordPress custom post type problems and provide effective solutions to ensure the seamless creation and management of custom post types on your website. Custom post types are powerful tools that allow you to organize and display content beyond traditional posts and pages. However, issues such as 404 errors, missing content, or improper custom post type registration can hinder the optimal presentation and functionality of your website. By mastering the art of fixing WordPress custom post type problems, you'll be empowered to maintain a well-structured and highly functional custom post type system that enhances your site's content management capabilities.

Identifying Custom Post Type Issues
Before exploring solutions, it's crucial to identify the signs of custom post type problems on your WordPress website. Common indications may include 404 page not found errors, missing custom post type content, or incorrect post type registration.

Solution:
1. *Review Permalink Settings*: Inspect your permalink settings to ensure they are correctly configured to display custom post type URLs.

2. ***Check Custom Post Type Registration***: Verify the registration code for custom post types and ensure it is correctly implemented.
3. ***Test Custom Post Type URLs***: Manually access custom post type URLs to check for any 404 errors or misdirects.

Resolving 404 Errors for Custom Post Types

404 errors for custom post types can occur due to incorrect permalinks or rewrite rules.

Solution:
1. ***Flush Rewrite Rules***: Reset the rewrite rules by navigating to "Settings" > "Permalinks" and saving the permalink settings again.
2. ***Verify Custom Post Type Slug***: Ensure the custom post type slug is unique and doesn't conflict with existing page or post slugs.
3. ***Check for Plugin Conflicts***: Temporarily deactivate plugins that might be interfering with custom post type URLs and test again.

Handling Missing Custom Post Type Content

Missing custom post type content can be caused by database issues or plugin conflicts.

Solution:
1. ***Verify Custom Post Type Data***: Check the database to ensure the custom post type content is present and hasn't been accidentally deleted.
2. ***Review Plugin Compatibility***: Confirm that any plugins associated with custom post types are compatible with your WordPress version.
3. ***Regenerate Custom Post Type Data***: If necessary, re-add the missing custom post type content to restore it to your website.

Fixing Custom Post Type Registration Problems

Issues with custom post type registration can result from coding errors or conflicting plugins.

Solution:

1. *Review Custom Post Type Code*: Inspect the code used to register custom post types and ensure it is accurate and free of syntax errors.
2. *Check for Plugin Conflicts*: Deactivate plugins one by one to determine if any are causing conflicts with custom post type registration.
3. *Use Custom Post Type Plugins*: Consider using dedicated plugins to register custom post types, as they often handle compatibility issues and simplify the process.

Troubleshooting Custom Post Type Templates

Custom post type templates may not display correctly due to theme conflicts or coding discrepancies.

Solution:

1. *Verify Template Hierarchy*: Ensure that your theme's template hierarchy includes specific templates for your custom post types.
2. *Check Template Files*: Review the code in custom post type template files for any errors or missing elements.
3. *Test with Default Theme*: Temporarily switch to a default WordPress theme to check if the issue is caused by a theme conflict.

Conclusion:

In conclusion, this chapter equips you with the expertise to fix WordPress custom post type problems effectively. By identifying custom post type issues, resolving 404 errors, handling missing content, fixing registration problems, and troubleshooting template display, you'll be well-prepared to maintain a well-organized and highly functional custom post type system on your WordPress website. Custom post types offer immense flexibility for content management, and the insights gained from this chapter will empower you to approach custom post type troubleshooting with confidence and efficiency. As you continue your WordPress troubleshooting journey, the knowledge from this chapter will serve as a valuable resource to optimize your custom post type setup, streamline content organization, and present a polished and engaging user experience, ultimately contributing to a versatile and successful WordPress site. Happy fixing WordPress custom post type problems!

CHAPTER 46: TROUBLESHOOTING WORDPRESS MEMORY EXHAUSTED ERRORS

In this critical chapter, we delve into the complexities of troubleshooting WordPress memory exhausted errors and provide effective solutions to ensure the smooth functioning and optimal performance of your website. Memory exhausted errors occur when WordPress consumes more PHP memory than allocated, leading to website crashes, white screens, or incomplete operations. These errors can be caused by resource-intensive plugins, large media files, or insufficient server memory. By mastering the art of troubleshooting WordPress memory exhausted errors, you'll be empowered to maintain a stable and efficient WordPress website that can handle various tasks and visitor traffic with ease.

Identifying Memory Exhausted Errors
Before exploring solutions, it's crucial to identify the signs of memory exhausted errors on your WordPress website. Common indications may include white screens of death, error messages, or incomplete page loads.

Solution:
1. **Enable WordPress Debugging**: Turn on WordPress debugging to view any memory exhausted errors or

warnings displayed on your website.

2. *Review Error Logs*: Inspect your server error logs to identify any memory-related issues that might be affecting your website.

3. *Check Server Resources*: Confirm if your server has sufficient memory available to handle the PHP memory requirements of your WordPress site.

Resolving Memory Exhausted Errors

Memory exhausted errors can be resolved through various methods, depending on their root causes.

Solution:

1. *Increase PHP Memory Limit*: Increase the PHP memory limit in your server settings to allocate more memory for your WordPress site.

2. *Deactivate Resource-Intensive Plugins*: Temporarily deactivate plugins known to be resource-intensive to check if they are causing the memory issue.

3. *Optimize Media Files*: Compress or resize large media files to reduce their memory footprint and improve website performance.

Implementing Caching and Performance Optimization

Caching and performance optimization techniques can help prevent memory exhausted errors by reducing server requests.

Solution:

1. *Use a Caching Plugin*: Implement a caching plugin to generate and serve cached versions of your WordPress pages, reducing the need for frequent PHP processing.

2. *Minimize External Requests*: Limit the number of external requests, such as third-party scripts or APIs, to reduce the server load and memory usage.

3. *Optimize Database Queries*: Optimize your WordPress database queries to reduce the strain on server resources during page rendering.

Checking Plugin and Theme Compatibility

Memory exhausted errors can arise due to conflicts between plugins or theme-related issues.

Solution:

1. **Update Plugins and Themes**: Ensure all your plugins and themes are up-to-date to maintain compatibility with the latest version of WordPress.
2. **Test Plugin Interactions**: Deactivate plugins one by one to identify if a specific plugin is causing memory issues when combined with others.
3. **Switch to Default Theme**: Temporarily switch to a default WordPress theme to determine if the issue is related to a theme conflict.

Consulting with Hosting Support

If you've exhausted all other options, seeking assistance from your hosting provider's support team may be necessary.

Solution:

1. **Contact Hosting Support**: Reach out to your hosting provider's support team for guidance on server-related memory issues.
2. **Inquire About Server Configuration**: Confirm if your server is optimized for WordPress, and inquire about any recommended settings or configurations.

Conclusion:

In conclusion, this chapter equips you with the expertise to troubleshoot WordPress memory exhausted errors effectively. By identifying memory exhausted errors, resolving the root causes, implementing caching and performance optimization, checking plugin and theme compatibility, and consulting with hosting support when needed, you'll be well-prepared to maintain a stable and efficient WordPress website. Memory management is crucial for website performance, and the insights gained from this chapter will empower you to approach memory exhausted error troubleshooting with confidence and efficiency. As you continue your WordPress troubleshooting journey, the knowledge from this chapter will serve as a valuable resource to optimize your website's memory usage, prevent future memory-related issues, and ensure a smooth and seamless user experience, ultimately contributing to a well-functioning and high-performing WordPress site. Happy troubleshooting WordPress memory exhausted errors!

CHAPTER 47: ADDRESSING WORDPRESS SITE HEALTH WARNINGS

In this crucial chapter, we explore the intricacies of addressing WordPress site health warnings and provide effective solutions to ensure your website meets the highest standards of performance, security, and functionality. WordPress introduced the Site Health feature to help website owners identify and rectify potential issues that might affect their site's operation and user experience. Site Health warnings can range from outdated PHP versions to insecure or incompatible plugins. By mastering the art of addressing WordPress site health warnings, you'll be empowered to maintain a healthy and well-optimized WordPress website that adheres to industry best practices.

Identifying Site Health Warnings
Before exploring solutions, it's essential to identify the site health warnings present on your WordPress website. Common indications may include PHP version warnings, insecure or outdated plugins, or issues with server configurations.

Solution:
1. *Access Site Health Page*: Navigate to the WordPress dashboard and go to "Tools" > "Site Health" to view the site health status and associated warnings.
2. *Review Warning Details*: Inspect each warning to understand its nature and potential impact on your website's performance and security.

3. *Check PHP Version*: Determine the PHP version currently used on your server to assess if it meets WordPress's recommended version.

Resolving PHP Version Warnings

Outdated PHP versions can pose security risks and may lead to performance issues with your WordPress website.

Solution:

1. *Update PHP Version*: Consult your hosting provider to update the PHP version to the latest recommended version compatible with your website.
2. *Verify Theme and Plugin Compatibility*: Ensure that your theme and plugins are compatible with the updated PHP version to prevent any conflicts.

Handling Plugin Incompatibility Warnings

Incompatible or outdated plugins can compromise your website's functionality and security.

Solution:

1. *Update Plugins*: Ensure all your plugins are up-to-date to maintain compatibility with the latest WordPress version.
2. *Replace Incompatible Plugins*: If a plugin is no longer maintained or causing conflicts, find alternative plugins with similar features and good compatibility.

Resolving Security-Related Warnings

Security-related warnings demand immediate attention to safeguard your WordPress website against potential vulnerabilities.

Solution:

1. *Install Security Plugins*: Utilize reputable security plugins to strengthen your website's defenses against common threats.
2. *Update WordPress Core*: Keep your WordPress core

updated to the latest stable version to receive security patches and enhancements.

3. **Secure User Accounts**: Enforce strong passwords, limit login attempts, and use two-factor authentication to protect user accounts.

Checking Server Configuration Warnings

Issues with your server's configurations can affect your website's performance and functionality.

Solution:

1. **Review Server Settings**: Inspect your server settings to ensure they meet WordPress's recommended configurations.
2. **Contact Hosting Support**: Reach out to your hosting provider's support team for assistance in optimizing server settings and resolving configuration issues.

Handling Database Warnings

Database-related warnings can indicate potential data integrity or performance problems.

Solution:

1. **Backup and Optimize Database**: Regularly back up your database and optimize it to ensure smooth performance and prevent data loss.
2. **Verify Database Connectivity**: Check database connection settings to ensure proper communication between WordPress and the database.

Conclusion:

In conclusion, this chapter equips you with the expertise to address WordPress site health warnings effectively. By identifying site health warnings, resolving PHP version issues, handling plugin incompatibility, resolving security-related concerns, checking server configurations, and addressing database warnings, you'll be well-prepared to maintain a healthy and well-optimized WordPress website. The Site Health feature is a valuable tool to keep your website in top shape, and the insights gained from this chapter will empower you to approach site health warning resolution with confidence and efficiency. As you continue your WordPress troubleshooting journey, the knowledge from this chapter will serve as a valuable resource to maintain a secure, high-performing, and compliant WordPress site, ultimately contributing to an exceptional user experience and the long-term success of your website. Happy addressing WordPress site health warnings!

CHAPTER 48: SOLVING WORDPRESS MULTISITE DOMAIN MAPPING ISSUES

In this critical chapter, we delve into the complexities of solving WordPress Multisite Domain Mapping issues and provide effective solutions to ensure the seamless configuration and functioning of domain mapping on your multisite network. WordPress Multisite allows you to manage multiple websites from a single installation, while domain mapping enables you to use custom domain names for each site in the network. However, domain mapping can present challenges such as misconfigured DNS settings, SSL certificate issues, or conflicts with plugins. By mastering the art of solving WordPress Multisite Domain Mapping issues, you'll be empowered to maintain a well-organized and accessible multisite network that delivers a unified user experience across custom domains.

Identifying Domain Mapping Issues
Before exploring solutions, it's crucial to identify the signs of domain mapping issues on your WordPress Multisite network. Common indications may include improper domain redirection, SSL certificate errors, or incorrect domain settings.

Solution:
1. *Review Domain Mapping Settings*: Inspect the domain mapping settings in your multisite network's WordPress dashboard to ensure they are configured correctly.

2. *Check Domain DNS Settings*: Verify the DNS settings for each custom domain to ensure they are pointing to the correct server.
3. *Test SSL Certificate*: Confirm that SSL certificates are correctly installed and valid for each custom domain.

Resolving Domain Redirection Problems

Domain redirection issues can occur when custom domains fail to direct to the correct site within the multisite network.

<u>Solution</u>:

1. *Check .htaccess Rules*: Review the .htaccess rules for your multisite installation to ensure proper domain redirection.
2. *Update Domain Mapping Plugin*: If you use a domain mapping plugin, make sure it is up-to-date and compatible with your WordPress version.
3. *Flush DNS Cache*: Clear the DNS cache on your computer and devices to ensure they pick up the correct domain mappings.

Fixing SSL Certificate Errors

SSL certificate errors can prevent secure connections to custom domains and may display warning messages to users.

<u>Solution</u>:

1. *Renew SSL Certificates*: Renew expired SSL certificates for custom domains to re-establish secure connections.
2. *Use Wildcard SSL Certificates*: Consider using wildcard SSL certificates to cover all subdomains within your multisite network.

Handling Conflicts with Plugins

Domain mapping issues can arise due to conflicts with other plugins in your multisite network.

<u>Solution</u>:

1. *Check Plugin Compatibility*: Ensure that all plugins in your multisite network are compatible with domain mapping and each other.
2. *Disable Conflicting Plugins*: Temporarily deactivate plugins one by one to identify if a specific plugin is causing domain mapping conflicts.
3. *Use Dedicated Domain Mapping Plugins*: Consider using specialized domain mapping plugins to minimize conflicts and streamline domain management.

Configuring Wildcard Subdomains

Wildcard subdomains allow automatic creation of subdomains for new sites in your multisite network.

Solution:

1. *Set Up Wildcard DNS Record*: Configure a wildcard DNS record that points all subdomains to your multisite installation's IP address.
2. *Update Server Settings*: Ensure that your server is configured to recognize wildcard subdomains and direct them to the correct site.

Consulting with Hosting Support

If domain mapping issues persist despite your efforts, seeking assistance from your hosting provider's support team may be necessary.

Solution:

1. *Contact Hosting Support*: Reach out to your hosting provider's support team for guidance on domain mapping issues and server configurations.
2. *Inquire About Multisite Setup*: Confirm if your hosting environment is optimized for WordPress Multisite and domain mapping.

Conclusion:

In conclusion, this chapter equips you with the expertise to solve WordPress Multisite Domain Mapping issues effectively.

By identifying domain mapping issues, resolving domain redirection problems, fixing SSL certificate errors, handling plugin conflicts, configuring wildcard subdomains, and consulting with hosting support when needed, you'll be well-prepared to maintain a smooth and seamless domain mapping experience in your multisite network. Domain mapping adds value to your multisite setup by providing a personalized user experience across custom domains, and the insights gained from this chapter will empower you to approach domain mapping troubleshooting with confidence and efficiency. As you continue your WordPress troubleshooting journey, the knowledge from this chapter will serve as a valuable resource to optimize your domain mapping setup, resolve domain-related issues, and ensure a cohesive and user-friendly multisite network, ultimately contributing to a unified and successful WordPress multisite experience. Happy solving WordPress Multisite Domain Mapping issues!

CHAPTER 49: RESOLVING WORDPRESS PHP ERRORS

In this crucial chapter, we explore the complexities of resolving WordPress PHP errors and provide effective solutions to ensure the stability and functionality of your WordPress website. PHP errors can occur due to coding mistakes, plugin or theme conflicts, or server configuration issues. These errors can lead to white screens, error messages, or broken functionality on your site. By mastering the art of resolving WordPress PHP errors, you'll be empowered to maintain a well-coded and error-free WordPress website that delivers a seamless user experience.

Identifying PHP Errors
Before exploring solutions, it's essential to identify the signs of PHP errors on your WordPress website. Common indications may include white screens of death, PHP parse errors, or error messages displaying on your site.

Solution:
1. *Enable WordPress Debugging*: Turn on WordPress debugging to display PHP errors and warnings on your website.
2. *Review Error Logs*: Inspect your server error logs to identify any PHP-related issues affecting your website.

Handling PHP Parse Errors
PHP parse errors occur when there are syntax errors in your WordPress theme or plugin files.

Solution:

1. **Review Code Changes**: If you recently made changes to your theme or plugin files, revert them to the previous version and check for errors.
2. **Use Code Editors**: Utilize code editors that highlight syntax errors to spot and correct issues in your code.

Fixing Plugin and Theme Conflicts

PHP errors can arise due to conflicts between plugins or theme-related issues.

Solution:

1. **Disable Conflicting Plugins**: Temporarily deactivate plugins one by one to identify if a specific plugin is causing PHP errors.
2. **Test with Default Theme**: Switch to a default WordPress theme to determine if the issue is related to a theme conflict.

Updating Outdated Code

Outdated code in themes or plugins can trigger PHP errors, especially after WordPress updates.

Solution:

1. **Update Themes and Plugins**: Ensure all your themes and plugins are up-to-date and compatible with the latest WordPress version.
2. **Consult Developers**: If a theme or plugin hasn't been updated for a long time, reach out to the developers for updates or alternatives.

Checking Server Compatibility

Issues with server configurations can cause PHP errors on your WordPress website.

Solution:

1. **Verify PHP Version**: Confirm that your server is running a compatible PHP version with the latest WordPress requirements.

2. *Adjust PHP Settings*: Modify PHP settings, such as memory_limit and max_execution_time, to match WordPress's recommended values.

Fixing Deprecated Functions
Deprecated PHP functions can trigger errors in newer PHP versions.

Solution:
1. *Review Deprecated Functions*: Identify and replace deprecated functions in your theme or plugin code with their updated equivalents.
2. *Check Plugin Updates*: Ensure that your plugins are using modern functions and are actively maintained by developers.

Resolving Syntax Errors in Custom Code
Custom PHP code snippets added to your website can contain syntax errors.

Solution:
1. *Check Custom Code*: Review any custom PHP code you've added to your theme's functions.php file or via plugins for syntax mistakes.
2. *Use Code Snippet Plugins*: Consider using code snippet plugins that provide syntax highlighting and error checking for your custom code.

Conclusion:
In conclusion, this chapter equips you with the expertise to resolve WordPress PHP errors effectively. By identifying PHP errors, handling PHP parse errors, fixing conflicts, updating outdated code, checking server compatibility, addressing deprecated functions, and resolving syntax errors in custom code, you'll be well-prepared to maintain a well-coded and error-free WordPress website. PHP is the backbone of WordPress, and the insights gained from this chapter will empower you to approach PHP error resolution with confidence and efficiency.

As you continue your WordPress troubleshooting journey, the knowledge from this chapter will serve as a valuable resource to optimize your PHP code, prevent future PHP-related issues, and ensure a seamless and reliable WordPress site, ultimately contributing to a positive user experience and the long-term success of your website. Happy resolving WordPress PHP errors!

CHAPTER 50: TROUBLESHOOTING WORDPRESS THEME UPDATE ISSUES

In this crucial chapter, we explore the intricacies of troubleshooting WordPress theme update issues and provide effective solutions to ensure a smooth and seamless updating process for your website's theme. Regularly updating your WordPress theme is essential for security, bug fixes, and access to new features. However, theme updates can sometimes lead to conflicts, broken layouts, or even website crashes. By mastering the art of troubleshooting WordPress theme update issues, you'll be empowered to maintain an up-to-date and well-functioning WordPress website that stays visually appealing and secure.

Identifying Theme Update Issues

Before exploring solutions, it's essential to identify the signs of theme update issues on your WordPress website. Common indications may include broken layouts, missing elements, or error messages after a theme update.

Solution:

1. *Review Recent Theme Changes*: If you encounter issues after updating your theme, review the changelog or update notes provided by the theme developer to

understand what changes were implemented.

2. **Check Theme Compatibility**: Ensure that the theme update is compatible with your current version of WordPress and other plugins.

Handling Theme Conflicts

Conflicts with other themes or plugins can arise after updating your WordPress theme.

Solution:

1. **Deactivate Conflicting Plugins**: Temporarily deactivate plugins one by one to identify if a specific plugin is causing conflicts with the updated theme.
2. **Switch to Default Theme**: Switch to a default WordPress theme to determine if the issue is related to a conflict with the previous theme.

Fixing Layout and Styling Issues

Theme updates can sometimes lead to layout or styling problems on your website.

Solution:

1. **Clear Browser Cache**: Clear your browser cache to ensure that you are viewing the latest version of your website after the theme update.
2. **Reset Theme Customizations**: If you've made extensive customizations to the theme's CSS or templates, try resetting them to see if it resolves any layout issues.

Restoring a Backup

In case the theme update causes significant issues, restoring a backup can be a viable solution.

Solution:

1. **Backup Your Website**: Before updating your theme, always create a full backup of your website, including the database and files.
2. **Restore the Backup**: If the theme update causes critical

errors that cannot be easily resolved, restore your website to the previous backup to revert the changes.

Reinstalling the Theme

If the theme update doesn't install correctly, reinstalling it can help resolve issues.

Solution:

1. *Download a Fresh Copy*: Download a fresh copy of the theme from the original source, ensuring it is the latest version.
2. *Reinstall the Theme*: Deactivate and delete the existing theme, then upload and activate the new version from the fresh copy you downloaded.

Contacting Theme Support

If all troubleshooting attempts fail, reaching out to the theme developer's support team can be beneficial.

Solution:

1. *Submit a Support Ticket*: Contact the theme developer's support team and provide them with detailed information about the issues you are experiencing after the theme update.
2. *Ask for Assistance*: Request their assistance in resolving the problems or inquire about any known issues related to the latest theme update.

Conclusion:

In conclusion, this chapter equips you with the expertise to troubleshoot WordPress theme update issues effectively. By identifying theme update issues, handling conflicts, fixing layout and styling problems, restoring backups if needed, reinstalling the theme, and seeking theme support when necessary, you'll be well-prepared to maintain a visually appealing and up-to-date WordPress website. Regular theme updates are essential for security and functionality, and the insights gained from this chapter will empower you to approach theme update troubleshooting with confidence and efficiency. As you continue your WordPress troubleshooting journey, the knowledge from this chapter will serve as a valuable resource to ensure seamless theme updates, prevent potential conflicts, and maintain a well-designed and functional WordPress website, ultimately contributing to a positive user experience and the long-term success of your online presence. Happy troubleshooting WordPress theme update issues!

CHAPTER 51: FIXING WORDPRESS SIDEBAR DISPLAY PROBLEMS

In this crucial chapter, we delve into the complexities of fixing WordPress sidebar display problems and provide effective solutions to ensure a well-organized and visually appealing sidebar on your WordPress website. Sidebars are essential components of many WordPress themes, used to display widgets, menus, and other important information. However, issues with sidebar display can arise due to conflicts with plugins or themes, coding errors, or CSS conflicts. By mastering the art of fixing WordPress sidebar display problems, you'll be empowered to maintain a professional and user-friendly website that showcases your content and functionality seamlessly.

Identifying Sidebar Display Issues

Before exploring solutions, it's essential to identify the signs of sidebar display problems on your WordPress website. Common indications may include missing sidebars, misplaced widgets, or overlapping elements in the sidebar area.

Solution:

1. *Review Theme Customizations*: If you encounter sidebar display issues, review any recent theme customizations or updates that may have caused the problem.

2. *Check Widget Settings*: Inspect the settings of your

widgets to ensure they are correctly configured and not causing conflicts.

Fixing Theme and Plugin Conflicts

Conflicts with themes or plugins can affect the display of your sidebar.

Solution:

1. *Deactivate Conflicting Plugins*: Temporarily deactivate plugins one by one to identify if a specific plugin is causing conflicts with the sidebar.
2. *Test with Default Theme*: Switch to a default WordPress theme to determine if the issue is related to a conflict with your current theme.

Correcting CSS Conflicts

CSS conflicts can lead to styling issues with your sidebar elements.

Solution:

1. *Use Browser Developer Tools*: Inspect the elements of your sidebar using browser developer tools to identify and correct CSS conflicts.
2. *Use Custom CSS*: If necessary, add custom CSS code to your theme's additional CSS section to adjust the styling of the sidebar.

Verifying Widget Settings

Improper widget settings can impact the display of your sidebar content.

Solution:

1. *Check Widget Visibility*: Review widget visibility settings to ensure widgets are set to display on the correct pages or posts.
2. *Inspect Widget Titles*: Verify that widget titles are correctly set and not overlapping with other elements in the sidebar.

Resolving Coding Errors

Coding errors in your theme or custom code snippets can lead to sidebar display problems.

Solution:

1. **Review Custom Code**: If you've added custom code snippets to your theme or plugins, review them for any coding errors.
2. **Validate HTML and PHP**: Use online validators to check for HTML and PHP errors in your theme templates and custom code.

Restoring Default Sidebar Layout

In some cases, restoring the default sidebar layout can resolve display problems.

Solution:

1. **Reset Widgets**: Remove all widgets from your sidebar and then re-add them one by one to ensure a clean layout.
2. **Use Theme Settings**: If your theme includes a built-in option to reset or restore the default sidebar layout, utilize this feature.

Conclusion:

In conclusion, this chapter equips you with the expertise to fix WordPress sidebar display problems effectively. By identifying sidebar display issues, fixing theme and plugin conflicts, correcting CSS conflicts, verifying widget settings, resolving coding errors, and restoring default sidebar layouts when needed, you'll be well-prepared to maintain a professional and visually appealing WordPress website. Sidebars play a significant role in organizing content and enhancing user experience, and the insights gained from this chapter will empower you to approach sidebar display troubleshooting with confidence and efficiency. As you continue your WordPress troubleshooting journey, the knowledge from this chapter will serve as a valuable resource to optimize your sidebar layout, prevent potential conflicts, and maintain a well-organized and user-friendly WordPress website, ultimately contributing to a positive user experience and the long-term success of your online presence. Happy fixing WordPress sidebar display problems!

CHAPTER 52: HANDLING WORDPRESS LOGIN REDIRECT ISSUES

In this critical chapter, we explore the intricacies of handling WordPress login redirect issues and provide effective solutions to ensure a smooth and secure login process for your website users. The login redirect process in WordPress is crucial for providing users with a seamless and personalized experience. However, login redirect issues can arise due to misconfigurations, conflicts with plugins, or security-related settings. By mastering the art of handling WordPress login redirect issues, you'll be empowered to maintain a user-friendly and secure login system that enhances the overall user experience on your WordPress website.

Identifying Login Redirect Problems
Before exploring solutions, it's essential to identify the signs of login redirect issues on your WordPress website. Common indications may include login loops, incorrect redirect destinations, or login page redirection errors.

Solution:
1. *Review Plugin Updates*: If you encounter login redirect issues after updating plugins, review the changelog or update notes to identify any potential conflicts.
2. *Check Custom Login Pages*: If you've customized the login page using plugins or custom code, verify that the customizations are not causing redirect problems.

Verifying Permalink Settings

Incorrect permalink settings can lead to login redirect problems in WordPress.

Solution:
1. *Update Permalink Structure*: Ensure that your website's permalink structure is set to a format that is compatible with your server and WordPress version.
2. *Reset Permalinks*: If login redirect issues persist, reset your permalinks by navigating to "Settings" > "Permalinks" and saving the changes.

Handling Conflict with Security Plugins

Security plugins can sometimes cause login redirect problems due to strict settings.

Solution:
1. *Adjust Security Plugin Settings*: Review the settings of your security plugins and adjust any login-related rules that might be causing redirects.
2. *Temporarily Disable Security Plugins*: Temporarily deactivate security plugins to see if the login redirect issues are resolved. However, only do this if you are confident in the security of your website during this period.

Clearing Browser Cache and Cookies

Browser cache and cookies can sometimes cause login redirect problems.

Solution:
1. *Clear Browser Cache*: Instruct your users to clear their browser cache and cookies to ensure they are not being redirected to outdated login pages.
2. *Use Incognito/Private Browsing Mode*: Advise users to use incognito or private browsing mode to bypass any caching issues temporarily.

Checking SSL Certificate Configuration

SSL certificate configuration can impact the login redirect process, especially when forced SSL is enabled.

Solution:

1. *Verify SSL Certificate*: Ensure that your SSL certificate is installed correctly and valid for your domain.
2. *Check SSL Settings*: Review your SSL settings, and if you are using a plugin to force SSL, verify that it's configured correctly.

Consulting with Hosting Support

If login redirect issues persist despite your efforts, contacting your hosting provider's support team may be necessary.

Solution:

1. *Contact Hosting Support*: Reach out to your hosting provider's support team and provide them with detailed information about the login redirect issues you are experiencing.
2. *Check Server Configuration*: Ask for assistance in verifying if your server configuration is causing login redirect problems and inquire about possible solutions.

Conclusion:

In conclusion, this chapter equips you with the expertise to handle WordPress login redirect issues effectively. By identifying login redirect problems, verifying permalink settings, handling conflicts with security plugins, clearing browser cache and cookies, checking SSL certificate configuration, and consulting with hosting support when needed, you'll be well-prepared to maintain a seamless and secure login process for your WordPress website. Login redirects are crucial for user experience and security, and the insights gained from this chapter will empower you to approach login redirect troubleshooting with confidence and efficiency. As you continue your WordPress troubleshooting journey, the knowledge from this chapter will serve as a valuable resource to optimize your login system, prevent potential conflicts, and maintain a user-friendly and secure WordPress website, ultimately contributing to a positive user experience and the long-term success of your online presence. Happy handling WordPress login redirect issues!

CHAPTER 53: TROUBLESHOOTING WORDPRESS CUSTOMIZER ERRORS

In this critical chapter, we delve into the intricacies of troubleshooting WordPress Customizer errors and provide effective solutions to ensure a smooth and seamless customization process for your WordPress website. The Customizer is a powerful built-in tool that allows users to customize various aspects of their website, including themes, colors, widgets, and more. However, errors in the Customizer can occur due to conflicts with themes or plugins, JavaScript issues, or server-related problems. By mastering the art of troubleshooting WordPress Customizer errors, you'll be empowered to offer a user-friendly and personalized website customization experience for your users.

Identifying Customizer Error Indications
Before exploring solutions, it's essential to identify the signs of Customizer errors on your WordPress website. Common indications may include a blank or unresponsive Customizer panel, error messages, or incomplete customization options.

Solution:
1. *Review Recent Changes*: If you encounter Customizer errors after making changes to your website, review

recent modifications to identify the potential cause.

2. *Check Plugin Updates*: Verify if any recently updated plugins may be conflicting with the Customizer functionality.

Handling Theme and Plugin Conflicts
Conflicts with themes or plugins can affect the functionality of the WordPress Customizer.

Solution:

1. *Deactivate Conflicting Plugins*: Temporarily deactivate plugins one by one to identify if a specific plugin is causing conflicts with the Customizer.

2. *Test with Default Theme*: Switch to a default WordPress theme to determine if the issue is related to a conflict with your current theme.

Clearing Browser Cache and Cookies
Browser cache and cookies can sometimes cause Customizer errors, especially after updates.

Solution:

1. *Clear Browser Cache*: Instruct users to clear their browser cache and cookies to ensure the Customizer loads the latest settings.

2. *Use Incognito/Private Browsing Mode*: Advise users to use incognito or private browsing mode to temporarily bypass any caching issues.

Checking JavaScript Errors
JavaScript errors can lead to Customizer functionality problems.

Solution:

1. *Inspect Browser Console*: Use the browser's developer tools to inspect the console for any JavaScript errors related to the Customizer.

2. *Review Custom JavaScript*: If you've added custom JavaScript to your website, review it for any syntax

errors that may affect the Customizer.

Verifying Server Configuration
Server-related issues can affect the loading and functionality of the Customizer.

Solution:
1. *Check Server Logs*: Review server logs to identify any potential server-related errors or resource limitations affecting the Customizer.
2. *Verify PHP and WordPress Versions*: Ensure that your server is running a compatible PHP version and the latest stable version of WordPress.

Testing with a Staging Site
If the Customizer errors persist, testing with a staging site can be helpful.

Solution:
1. *Set Up Staging Site*: Create a staging site using a staging plugin or your hosting provider's staging feature.
2. *Test Customizer on Staging*: Replicate the Customizer settings and content on the staging site to isolate and resolve any issues.

Conclusion:
In conclusion, this chapter equips you with the expertise to troubleshoot WordPress Customizer errors effectively. By identifying Customizer error indications, handling theme and plugin conflicts, clearing browser cache and cookies, checking JavaScript errors, verifying server configuration, and testing with a staging site when necessary, you'll be well-prepared to offer a seamless and user-friendly customization experience for your WordPress website users. The Customizer is a valuable tool for website personalization, and the insights gained from this chapter will empower you to approach Customizer error troubleshooting with confidence and efficiency. As you continue your WordPress troubleshooting journey, the knowledge from

this chapter will serve as a valuable resource to optimize the Customizer, prevent potential conflicts, and maintain a well-customized and engaging WordPress website, ultimately contributing to a positive user experience and the long-term success of your online presence. Happy troubleshooting WordPress Customizer errors!

CHAPTER 54: RESOLVING WORDPRESS THUMBNAIL AND FEATURED IMAGE ISSUES

In this crucial chapter, we explore the intricacies of resolving WordPress thumbnail and featured image issues and provide effective solutions to ensure a visually appealing and well-organized website. Thumbnails and featured images are essential for showcasing content effectively, but issues may arise due to misconfigurations, theme conflicts, or media library problems. By mastering the art of resolving WordPress thumbnail and featured image issues, you'll be empowered to maintain a professional and engaging presentation of your content on your WordPress website.

Identifying Thumbnail and Featured Image Problems
Before exploring solutions, it's essential to identify the signs of thumbnail and featured image issues on your WordPress website. Common indications may include missing or incorrect thumbnails, featured images not displaying correctly, or distorted image appearances.

Solution:
1. *Review Media Library*: If you encounter thumbnail and featured image issues, review your media library to ensure images are properly uploaded and assigned.

2. *Check Theme Settings*: Verify if your theme supports featured images and if there are any specific settings related to thumbnails and featured images.

Regenerating Thumbnails

Regenerating thumbnails can resolve issues with image sizes not displaying correctly.

<u>Solution</u>:
1. *Use a Regeneration Plugin*: Install and use a thumbnail regeneration plugin to regenerate image sizes for existing media files.
2. *Reupload Problematic Images*: If specific images still have issues, reupload them to the media library and set them as featured images again.

Handling Theme and Plugin Conflicts

Conflicts with themes or plugins can affect thumbnail and featured image functionality.

<u>Solution</u>:
1. *Deactivate Conflicting Plugins*: Temporarily deactivate plugins one by one to identify if a specific plugin is causing conflicts with image display.
2. *Test with Default Theme*: Switch to a default WordPress theme to determine if the issue is related to a conflict with your current theme.

Checking File Permissions

Incorrect file permissions can lead to issues with image uploads and display.

<u>Solution</u>:
1. *Review File Permissions*: Verify that the directories and files in your WordPress installation have appropriate permissions (usually 755 for directories and 644 for files).
2. *Set Correct Permissions*: Use an FTP client or your

hosting control panel to adjust file permissions if needed.

Checking Image File Types

Image file types can affect thumbnail and featured image display.

Solution:

1. *Use Supported File Types*: Ensure that you are using supported image file types such as JPEG, PNG, or GIF for thumbnails and featured images.
2. *Convert Images*: If you are using unsupported file types, convert them to a supported format before uploading.

Verifying Image Dimensions and Quality

Incorrect image dimensions or quality settings can lead to display issues.

Solution:

1. *Follow Theme Guidelines*: Check your theme documentation for recommended image dimensions and quality settings for thumbnails and featured images.
2. *Resize and Compress Images*: Use image editing software to resize images to the recommended dimensions and compress them to a reasonable file size.

Conclusion:

In conclusion, this chapter equips you with the expertise to resolve WordPress thumbnail and featured image issues effectively. By identifying thumbnail and featured image problems, regenerating thumbnails, handling theme and plugin conflicts, checking file permissions, verifying image file types, and ensuring appropriate image dimensions and quality, you'll be well-prepared to maintain a visually appealing and engaging WordPress website. Thumbnails and featured images are critical for content presentation, and the insights gained from this chapter will empower you to approach image issue resolution with confidence and efficiency. As you continue your WordPress troubleshooting journey, the knowledge from this chapter will serve as a valuable resource to optimize your image display, prevent potential conflicts, and maintain a well-organized and visually captivating WordPress website, ultimately contributing to a positive user experience and the long-term success of your online presence. Happy resolving WordPress thumbnail and featured image issues!

CHAPTER 55: FIXING WORDPRESS MENU DISPLAY PROBLEMS

In this critical chapter, we delve into the intricacies of fixing WordPress menu display problems and provide effective solutions to ensure a well-organized and user-friendly navigation experience on your WordPress website. Menus play a crucial role in guiding visitors to various sections of your site, but issues with menu display can arise due to misconfigurations, theme conflicts, or plugin-related problems. By mastering the art of fixing WordPress menu display problems, you'll be empowered to offer a seamless and intuitive navigation system for your website users.

Identifying Menu Display Issues

Before exploring solutions, it's essential to identify the signs of menu display problems on your WordPress website. Common indications may include missing menus, incorrect menu items, broken links, or menu items not displaying in the correct order.

Solution:

1. *Check Menu Settings*: If you encounter menu display issues, review the menu settings in the WordPress dashboard to ensure they are correctly configured.
2. *Review Theme Customizations*: Verify if recent theme customizations or updates have affected the menu display on your website.

Verifying Menu Locations and Assignments
Menu locations and assignments can impact the visibility of menus on different pages.

Solution:
1. *Assign Menus to Correct Locations*: Ensure that you've assigned the appropriate menus to the correct menu locations defined by your theme.
2. *Check Page-Specific Menus*: If using page-specific menus, verify that they are assigned to the correct pages or posts.

Handling Theme and Plugin Conflicts
Conflicts with themes or plugins can affect the functionality of WordPress menus.

Solution:
1. *Deactivate Conflicting Plugins*: Temporarily deactivate plugins one by one to identify if a specific plugin is causing conflicts with the menu display.
2. *Test with Default Theme*: Switch to a default WordPress theme to determine if the issue is related to a conflict with your current theme.

Clearing Browser Cache and Cookies
Browser cache and cookies can sometimes cause menu display problems, especially after updates.

Solution:
1. *Clear Browser Cache*: Instruct your users to clear their browser cache and cookies to ensure they are viewing the latest menu changes.
2. *Use Incognito/Private Browsing Mode*: Advise users to use incognito or private browsing mode to temporarily bypass any caching issues.

Checking CSS and Styling
CSS conflicts or improper styling can lead to issues with menu

appearance and layout.

Solution:
1. *Use Browser Developer Tools*: Inspect the menu elements using browser developer tools to identify and correct CSS conflicts.
2. *Use Custom CSS*: If necessary, add custom CSS code to your theme's additional CSS section to adjust the styling of the menu.

Verifying Custom Menu Items
Custom menu items may cause display problems if not set up correctly.

Solution:
1. *Review Custom Menu URLs*: Check the URLs of custom menu items to ensure they are correctly pointing to the desired destinations.
2. *Check Labels and Titles*: Verify that the labels and titles of custom menu items are accurately representing the linked content.

Conclusion:
In conclusion, this chapter equips you with the expertise to fix WordPress menu display problems effectively. By identifying menu display issues, verifying menu locations and assignments, handling theme and plugin conflicts, clearing browser cache and cookies, checking CSS and styling, and verifying custom menu items, you'll be well-prepared to maintain a seamless and user-friendly navigation system for your WordPress website. Menus are essential for user navigation, and the insights gained from this chapter will empower you to approach menu display troubleshooting with confidence and efficiency. As you continue your WordPress troubleshooting journey, the knowledge from this chapter will serve as a valuable resource to optimize your menus, prevent potential conflicts, and maintain a well-organized and intuitive WordPress website, ultimately

contributing to a positive user experience and the long-term success of your online presence. Happy fixing WordPress menu display problems!

CHAPTER 56: TROUBLESHOOTING WORDPRESS CHILD THEME ISSUES

In this critical chapter, we explore the intricacies of troubleshooting WordPress child theme issues and provide effective solutions to ensure a smooth and efficient child theme implementation on your WordPress website. Child themes are essential for making customizations while preserving the parent theme's core functionality. However, issues with child themes can arise due to misconfigurations, code conflicts, or incorrect implementation. By mastering the art of troubleshooting WordPress child theme issues, you'll be empowered to confidently customize your website while maintaining a stable and up-to-date foundation.

Identifying Child Theme Issues

Before exploring solutions, it's essential to identify the signs of child theme issues on your WordPress website. Common indications may include broken layouts, missing customizations, or errors in custom code.

Solution:

1. *Review Child Theme Files*: If you encounter child theme issues, review the child theme files to ensure they are correctly set up and properly connected to the parent

theme.

2. ***Check Custom Code***: Verify if any custom code in the child theme is causing conflicts or errors.

Verifying Parent Theme Compatibility

Child themes rely on the parent theme's functionality, so compatibility is crucial.

Solution:

1. ***Update Parent Theme***: Ensure that both the parent theme and child theme are using the latest versions.
2. ***Check Theme Documentation***: Review the parent theme's documentation to ensure that customizations are compatible with the latest updates.

Handling Customization Conflicts

Conflicts with customizations between the parent and child themes can lead to display and functionality problems.

Solution:

1. ***Isolate Custom Code***: Isolate the custom code in the child theme to identify if it's causing conflicts with the parent theme.
2. ***Test Individual Customizations***: Temporarily disable individual customizations in the child theme to pinpoint the conflicting code.

Clearing Caches and Regenerating Assets

Caching and asset regeneration can sometimes affect the display of child theme customizations.

Solution:

1. ***Clear Caches***: Instruct your users to clear their browser cache and any caching plugins to ensure they are viewing the latest child theme customizations.
2. ***Regenerate Assets***: Use caching plugins or your hosting control panel to regenerate CSS and JavaScript assets to reflect the latest changes.

Reviewing File Permissions

Incorrect file permissions can cause issues with child theme file access and functionality.

Solution:

1. *Verify File Permissions*: Check the file permissions of the child theme files to ensure they have the appropriate read and write permissions.
2. *Adjust File Permissions*: Use an FTP client or your hosting control panel to modify file permissions if needed.

Checking PHP Compatibility

Child themes may encounter issues if the PHP version is not compatible.

Solution:

1. *Verify PHP Version*: Check your hosting environment's PHP version and ensure it meets the minimum requirements of the parent and child themes.
2. *Update PHP Version*: If using an outdated PHP version, update it to a compatible version.

Conclusion:

In conclusion, this chapter equips you with the expertise to troubleshoot WordPress child theme issues effectively. By identifying child theme issues, verifying parent theme compatibility, handling customization conflicts, clearing caches and regenerating assets, reviewing file permissions, and checking PHP compatibility, you'll be well-prepared to implement and customize child themes confidently on your WordPress website. Child themes offer a powerful way to customize your website without affecting the parent theme, and the insights gained from this chapter will empower you to approach child theme troubleshooting with confidence and efficiency. As you continue your WordPress troubleshooting journey, the knowledge from this chapter will serve as a valuable resource to optimize your child theme customizations, prevent potential conflicts, and maintain a stable and flexible WordPress website, ultimately contributing to a positive user experience and the long-term success of your online presence. Happy troubleshooting WordPress child theme issues!

CHAPTER 57: ADDRESSING WORDPRESS RSS FEED VALIDATION ERRORS

In this crucial chapter, we explore the intricacies of addressing WordPress RSS feed validation errors and provide effective solutions to ensure smooth syndication and distribution of your website's content. RSS feeds are a fundamental feature of WordPress, allowing users and other platforms to access your content easily. However, issues with RSS feed validation can occur due to malformed XML, plugin conflicts, or misconfigurations. By mastering the art of addressing WordPress RSS feed validation errors, you'll be empowered to maintain a well-formatted and accessible RSS feed for your website, enhancing content visibility and reach.

Identifying RSS Feed Validation Errors
Before exploring solutions, it's essential to identify the signs of RSS feed validation errors on your WordPress website. Common indications may include feed parsing errors, missing or incorrect tags, or invalid character encoding.

Solution:
1. *Use Feed Validators*: Employ online feed validation tools to identify specific issues and errors in your RSS feed.
2. *Check Browser and Feed Reader Compatibility*: Test your RSS feed in different browsers and feed readers to ensure compatibility.

Validating XML Structure
Malformed XML can lead to RSS feed validation errors.

Solution:
1. *Check for XML Errors*: Use XML validation tools to detect any syntax errors in your RSS feed's XML structure.
2. *Review Custom Code*: If you've added custom code to your RSS feed, review it for any XML syntax issues that may affect validation.

Handling Plugin Conflicts
Conflicts with plugins can affect the generation and validation of your RSS feed.

Solution:
1. *Deactivate Plugins*: Temporarily deactivate plugins one by one to identify if a specific plugin is causing conflicts with the RSS feed.
2. *Check Feed-Related Plugins*: Focus on plugins specifically related to RSS feed generation and syndication.

Reviewing Feed Settings
Misconfigurations in feed settings can cause validation errors.

Solution:
1. *Verify Feed Settings*: Review your WordPress settings related to RSS feeds and ensure they are correctly configured.
2. *Test with Different Settings*: Experiment with different feed settings to identify if a specific configuration is causing validation errors.

Handling Special Characters
Invalid character encoding can lead to issues with RSS feed validation.

Solution:
1. ***Use Proper Character Encoding***: Ensure that your RSS feed uses valid character encoding, such as UTF-8, to support special characters.
2. ***Check Content Input***: Review content inputs to prevent the use of unsupported characters that may disrupt validation.

Updating WordPress and Plugins

Outdated WordPress or plugin versions may result in RSS feed validation errors.

Solution:
1. ***Update WordPress Core***: Ensure that your WordPress installation is running the latest stable version.
2. ***Update Plugins***: Keep all your plugins up to date to ensure compatibility and improved feed functionality.

Conclusion:

In conclusion, this chapter equips you with the expertise to address WordPress RSS feed validation errors effectively. By identifying RSS feed validation errors, validating XML structure, handling plugin conflicts, reviewing feed settings, handling special characters, and updating WordPress and plugins, you'll be well-prepared to maintain a well-formatted and accessible RSS feed for your WordPress website. RSS feeds are essential for content syndication and distribution, and the insights gained from this chapter will empower you to approach RSS feed validation troubleshooting with confidence and efficiency. As you continue your WordPress troubleshooting journey, the knowledge from this chapter will serve as a valuable resource to optimize your RSS feed, prevent potential validation errors, and enhance the visibility and reach of your content, ultimately contributing to a positive user experience and the long-term success of your online presence. Happy addressing WordPress RSS feed validation errors!

ABOUT THE AUTHOR

Tasvir Mahmood

Meet Tasvir Mahmood, a seasoned WordPress expert hailing from the vibrant city of Chittagong, Bangladesh. Currently residing in the bustling capital, Dhaka, Tasvir's journey is a testament to his unwavering passion for WordPress and his dedication to crafting exceptional online experiences.

With a remarkable journey spanning over 7 years in the realm of WordPress, Tasvir's expertise shines through his extensive portfolio of over 1000 WordPress websites. His keen eye for detail and innovative solutions have propelled him to the forefront of the industry. Tasvir's mastery over WordPress troubleshooting has been honed through years of hands-on experience, transforming him into a go-to authority for resolving the most intricate website issues.

Beyond the realm of coding and troubleshooting, Tasvir's commitment to the WordPress community shines brightly. His insights and contributions have earned him a reputation as a reliable guide in the dynamic world of WordPress. Whether it's crafting visually appealing websites or navigating the complexities of coding, Tasvir's journey is an inspiration to those seeking to harness the full potential of WordPress.

Embark on a journey through the world of WordPress alongside Tasvir Mahmood, and uncover a wealth of knowledge and experience that only a true enthusiast and seasoned professional can offer.

For more info about him visit his website: www.tasvirwebsolutions.com

BOOKS BY THIS AUTHOR

The Wordpress Security Handbook: Protecting Your Site From Attacks

The WordPress Security Handbook is a comprehensive guide that covers all aspects of securing a WordPress site. With 30 chapters, it covers everything from an introduction to WordPress security, to understanding the different threats that can affect your site, to implementing best practices for managing user accounts and passwords. One of the key topics covered in the book is the importance of keeping WordPress core and plugins up to date. Outdated software can be a major security risk and can leave your site vulnerable to attacks. The book explains how to check for updates, and provides tips on how to ensure that updates don't cause any compatibility issues.

Wordpress Performance Optimization: Speeding Up Your Site For Better User Experience

"WordPress Performance Optimization: Speeding Up Your Site for Better User Experience" covers a wide range of important topics related to optimizing WordPress performance. The book covers topics such as optimizing website speed, improving user experience, and enhancing site security. It also discusses how to manage user permissions, secure WordPress login, and prevent spam and comments on the site.

www.ingramcontent.com/pod-product-compliance
Lightning Source LLC
Chambersburg PA
CBHW071109050326
40690CB00008B/1169